Shooting the Franklin

*This book is dedicated to
the memory of John Hawkins,
whose enthusiasm for adventure
never waned.*

JOHNSON DEAN

Shooting the Franklin

Early canoeing on Tasmania's wild rivers

SHOOTING THE FRANKLIN
Early Canoeing on Tasmania's Wild Rivers

Johnson Dean

ISBN 0-9581744-0-7

Photographs from the Hawkins–Dean collection unless otherwise acknowledged

Maps produced using digital topographic data provided by and with the permission of the Land Management Branch, Department of Primary Industries, Water and Environment

Illustrations by Stephanie Dean

Graphic design by Julie Hawkins, e.g. design

Printed in Australia by Brown Prior Anderson

FOREWORD

I had no idea, when I drove up to the little white farmhouse beside the Liffey River in northern Tasmania in 1973 that its welcoming owner, John Dean, had been in the first party to canoe down the Franklin River 14 years earlier.

In fact, like most Tasmanians then, I had never heard of the Franklin. But I bought the house and have been there ever since.

Nor had I had any idea, as the junior doctor holding his retractor in the Alice Springs Hospital in 1969, that Dr John Hawkins had also been a Franklin pioneering canoeist.

Not until Paul Smith asked me to join him for a rafting trip down the river in 1976 did I realise that my life had already crossed currents with the earlier Franklin adventurers.

Yet, while the story of the thousands of people who campaigned and were even gaoled during the 'No Dams' protests to save the Franklin River in the early 1980s made world headlines, the story of the first canoeists was largely forgotten.

Now, here are John Dean's exciting, charming and, at times, harrowing accounts of the intrepid young men who set off on the first trips down the Franklin as well as the King, Pieman and middle Gordon rivers. The Huck Finn style trials on the South Esk River upstream of Launceston are also an amusing prelude.

John's stories and photographs are an important contribution to the bookshelf of Tasmania's history. His energy-packed book is also the ideal replacement for the gelignite and shotguns of old, in every modern Franklin rafter's pack.

BOB BROWN
Liffey 2002

RIVER LOCATIONS

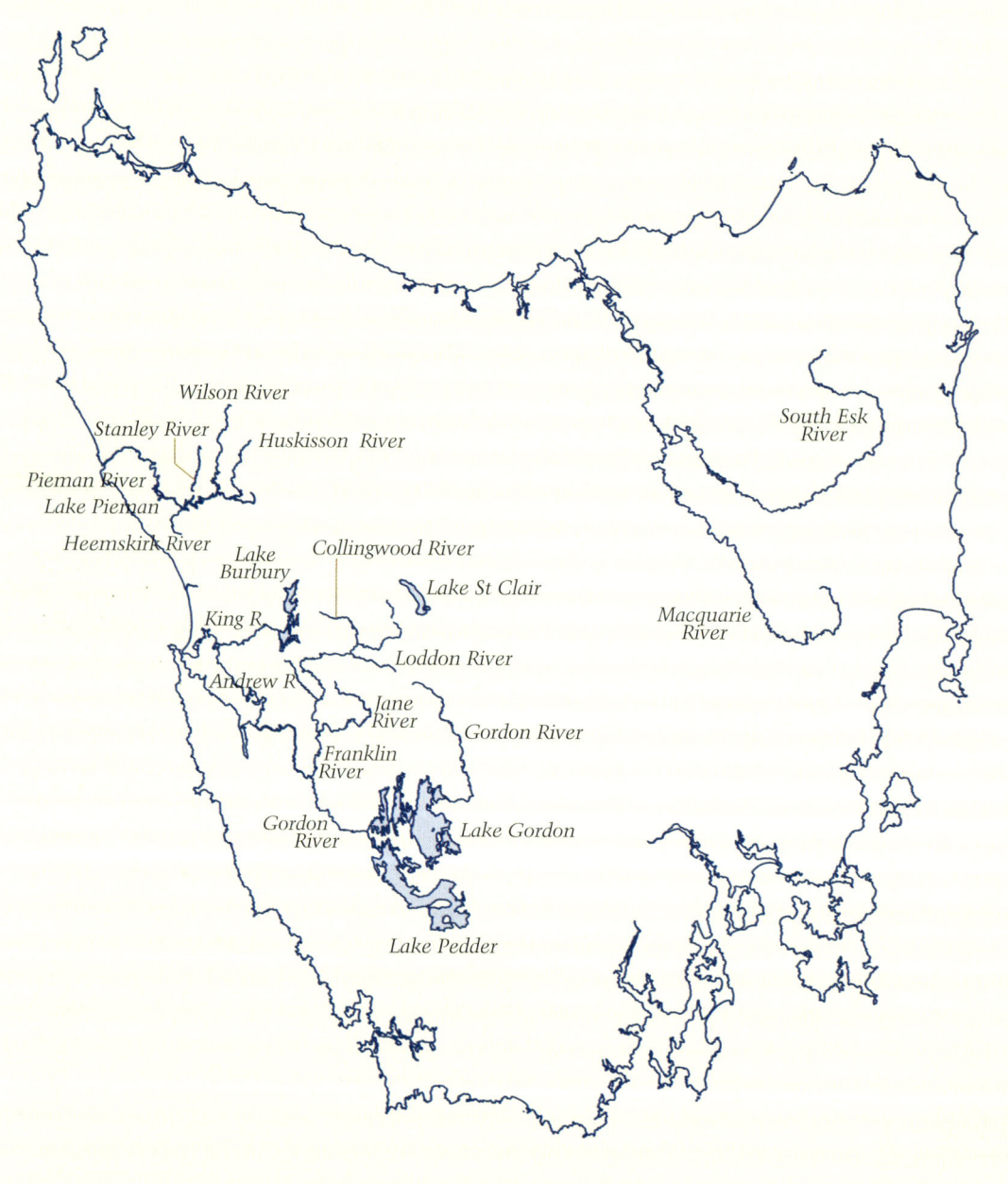

Wilson River

Stanley River   Huskisson River

Pieman River
Lake Pieman

Heemskirk River   Lake Burbury   Collingwood River

South Esk River

Lake St Clair

King R.

Macquarie River

Andrew R.

Loddon River

Jane River

Gordon River

Franklin River

Gordon River   Lake Gordon

Lake Pedder

CONTENTS

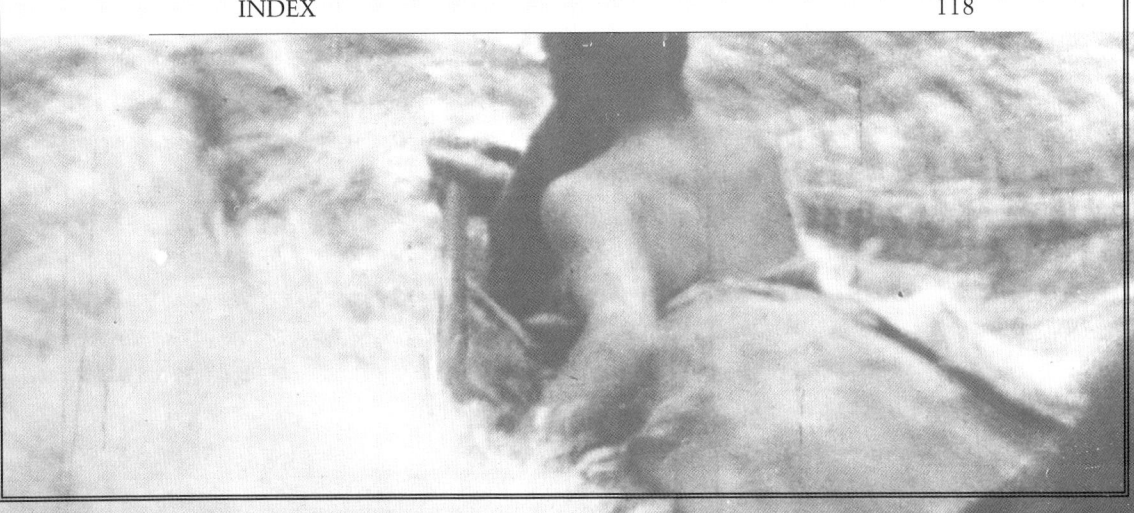

ACKNOWLEDGEMENTS

I wish to thank the following for their assistance and encouragement in preparing this book:

John Hawkins' wife Kay for making available stills from his movies and personal maps, and his sister June Gee for the King River diary.

Senator Bob Brown, Bruce and Karen Crawford, Henry Crocker, Tony Davidson, Liz Dean, Helen Gee, June Gee, John Gibb, Professor Andrew Osborn, Clive Tilsley, Joan Tilt, Jeff Weston and Max Wilson.

My family, Geoff and Jo, Malcolm, Annette and Thomas, for their practical assistance, particularly with the computer. A special thanks to my wife Stephanie for typing my awful handwriting and checking script, and, above all, for her patience and encouragement, without which this book would not have seen the light of day.

Hawkins' observations.

INTRODUCTION

Life in Evandale just prior to World War II and in the early forties was very different from today. Young people had to find their own amusements, something I had no problem doing, especially in summertime when the nearby South Esk River beckoned for swimming and canoeing.

From an early age I learned to be independent. Being the second youngest of a family of six ensured this. In our family it was understood from an early age that it was our own responsibility to avoid hazards if we wished to survive. This I managed to do most of the time. When I was seven, however, I picked up a pair of old rusty sheep shears to cut something. The blades were tied tightly together with a piece of string and, not having a knife handy, I used a lighted match to burn this through. What I didn't know was that they were spring-loaded and, as soon as I did this, they flew open and one side penetrated my right eye as far as the retina. Now I have little sight in that eye.

Evandale was a quiet village of just a few hundred souls, most of whom were employed on surrounding farms, particularly at harvest time. When my father started sawmilling at the rear of the old stables at *Blenheim* the serenity of the village was somewhat shattered. Other sawmillers thought he was mad getting logs carted from as far away as English Town. What I now find interesting is that just prior to World War II he also milled some Huon pine logs which were railed from Strahan. About this time R.J. Howard's men were operating from Wattle Camp (later Jane River Hut) on the Franklin River.[1] Perhaps my father's logs were some of these! During the war the three-foot-wide Huon pine boards were bought by the Defence Department for pattern making.

School was not the happiest of times for me, although things improved at Launceston High School. Getting to a town school, however, was not easy. We first had to ride our bikes to the railway station at Western Junction. Once or twice I attached a sail from our canoe to the bike to make life easier. Unfortunately there were head winds each time so I abandoned the idea. One morning I met the local policeman on his motorbike and he just looked in amazement. There was a regular mail car but we couldn't afford the fare of sixpence (five cents).

But when I compared myself to the McKinnell family I didn't complain. The McKinnell boys all lived at Nile and, after milking the cows each morning, had to ride 14 kilometres to Western Junction station over a corrugated gravel road often in head winds. When they returned home in the early evening the cows had to be milked again. On reaching Launceston station we walked about a kilometre with a case of books to school. If the train was on time we only missed half the first period. Whether I would have been a better student without the aforementioned handicaps is doubtful.

In the end, the most valuable asset I acquired were close friends. Without them few of the adventures which followed would have eventuated.

Once bitten

One look at the forlorn canoe with its wrinkled skin and cracked paintwork should have been enough to convince us it would never last the distance. Any lingering doubt was dispelled when, lifted by one end, it showed every sign of a broken back. Obviously major surgery was required. The one big problem was that this would have to be accomplished in a matter of hours. The train to take us to Fingal, the launching place for our first canoeing venture, was due to leave that evening. Panic set in.

Above: Flea the dog took part in our early canoeing adventures.
Opposite: Negotiating shallow rapids on the South Esk above Avoca, 1947.

We worked furiously all day under a hot December sun to replace most of the skeleton and by late afternoon that part of the task had been completed. All that remained to be done was to waterproof the canvas with an oil-based paint. Unfortunately, all such paint had been requisitioned for the war effort and we could only obtain one small tin of green camouflage paint, which we sparingly applied. Perhaps we were not entirely confident about this because we agreed that it might be a good idea to have a trial run, especially as the local river was only a short distance from Evandale railway station, our departure point.

Jeff Weston, the proud owner, launched his refurbished vessel onto the nearby South Esk River, hopped in, and commenced to paddle into deeper water. The other members of the party looked on from the old wooden bridge. Everything seemed normal until the river slowly turned green for yards around the canoe. He couldn't understand the reason for our laughter until he noticed the green expanse of water behind him and realised with alarm that the 'waterproofing' paint was fast dissolving! Worse still, the canoe was taking water. With departure time fast approaching the only solution was to include a good sized billy for baling.

The South Esk flows quite close to Evandale and from an early age my older brother Ray and I would launch our homemade canoe and paddle upstream, usually as far as the first rapids, a distance of about a mile. When my close mate John Hawkins stayed at our place in the school holidays of 1944 we ventured further up the river and, after battling the swift current, decided that it would be a better idea to put the canoe in somewhere higher up and go with the flow. The furthest easily accessible departure point was Fingal, a distance of about fifty-five miles by road or rail. In reality the only practical choice was the latter. To go by road would have taken all of one month's wartime petrol ration of four gallons (10 litres).

It was probably no coincidence that amongst my school friends the ones most interested in the first canoeing ventures were rowers. Jeff Weston, Bruce Rose and I were members of the 1945 Launceston High School rowing crew. We were all reasonably good swimmers, but not so Hawkins. Never having had much opportunity to learn to swim he was not happy in the water— not the ideal criterion for a canoeist. Nevertheless in the end he was the keenest of all, never missing an opportunity

Portaging the primitive home-made canoes over the only log jam on the South Esk journey. PHOTO: WILSON

to revisit the more spectacular rivers and refusing to let fear of water take precedence over his love for the sport.

My friendship with John Hawkins began over lunch at the Anzac Hostel in 1943 when he asked about my school. He was completing his third year at Launceston Technical College after which he would transfer to High School in order to study a foreign language for matriculation. We were to be in the same class. On completing his last year at Tech he obtained a maximum possible result of nine credits. It is probably surprising that we became close friends because my academic achievements were mediocre at best. Nevertheless we soon discovered common interests. One of these was hunting and shooting.

In the hilly country around Lebrina, where his father was the schoolmaster, Hawkins worked on a system to improve accuracy when shooting rabbits on the other side of wide gullies. The idea was to lie on his back and steady the rifle barrel between raised knees. He claimed great success with this method until on one occasion he misjudged the length of the barrel and the bullet grazed his kneecap. He was still limping two days later when he returned to school and when he confessed to what he had done was greeted with howls of derision. He took this with good humour and the incident was forgotten until I reminded him of it three years later when he won a Blue for small bore rifle shooting at Melbourne University, obviously using a different technique!

Jeff Weston's background made him the ideal companion. Brought up on a mixed farm just outside Lilydale he had 'done it tough'. His parents often relied on him to provide food for the table and he would trap or shoot rabbits or catch fish in the stream that ran through the property. While not a regular practice, 'tickling' fish, that is, catching fish by hand, was one means of doing this. One day he and school friend Max Wilson were testing their skill near Lilydale Falls when one of them grabbed by the tail what they thought was an eel, but instead pulled out a snake. Needless to say, he soon let go! Unlike Hawkins and me, Weston had been a Boy Scout and this stood him in good stead when it came to living outdoors. We had to learn the hard way.

Then I heard of someone who had already canoed the South Esk from Fingal. His name was Jack Cox. He invited me to inspect the large Canadian canoe he had designed and built to suit his requirements for annual holidays on the South Esk. A set of golf clubs was an essential part of his gear. He once came down the river during a major flood, enabling him to take many short cuts around trees and over the tops of fences. He completed the journey from Fingal to Launceston in three days, or less than half the time taken at normal river levels. His stories made me all the keener to try it myself.

Weston persuaded Bruce Rose to accompany him. Rose was a brainy type who went on to become a civil engineer. Then there was a hitch. Because Hawkins couldn't swim his father wouldn't agree to him taking part and, while not happy with this decision, he reluctantly bowed out. Syd Smith, a fellow classmate, was talked into accompanying Rose. They decided to use

Rose's older brother's canoe which was more robust than Weston's but even less stable than mine. It lacked stability because of insufficient beam. Both were under twelve feet (four metres) long, designed along Canadian lines, with a framework of steamed hardwood laths, fixed together equidistantly. Mine was covered with ageing painted hessian. Rose's suffered from large cracks, through being stored on top of a henhouse for many years. Someone came up with the suggestion that tar might be the remedy for our problem. After scrounging some from the local council road overseer it was liberally applied to the upturned canoe, already aboard the open rail wagon. This seemed to be a good idea at the time, but we paid for our hasty decision later.

In those days getting ourselves and canoes to the starting point was in itself an undertaking. The goods train arrived at Evandale station an hour late, and the guard was not a happy man. He insisted that my dog, Flea, be on a lead before we could take him with us. This we considered unreasonable as the carriage allocated to us was commonly known as a 'dog box' but we grudgingly complied by tying a piece of string around Flea's neck. The train hooked onto the truck containing our canoes and rattled south to Conara, arriving three hours later. There we waited until midnight when our carriage was shunted onto the Fingal Valley line to make up a train consisting of our carriage and truck and a few empty wagons. While waiting to change trains we attempted to sleep but arrangements were far from commodious. The two lucky ones slept on the horsehair seats, the third person on the floor and the unlucky fourth balanced on a narrow, netted luggage rack above. Flea squeezed in under a seat.

First light revealed the pale green foliage of willows defining the course of the distant South Esk. Where the line came alongside, we were able to look down onto the surprisingly wide, fast flowing river which promised some exciting canoeing. We were not to be disappointed.

At Fingal we obtained loaves of bread from the local store to add to our meagre food supply. During the last weeks of the school year each member of the party had undertaken to scrounge whatever tinned supplies he could from the family food ration. This, together with spare clothing, sleeping bags and anything else that could be squeezed in, was now packed into groundsheet-lined apple cases, one of which doubled as a seat for the bowman in each canoe. The sternman sat high on the rear deck. It didn't seem to occur to us that a lower centre of gravity would be more sensible; comfort was more important!

Needless to say we capsized many times, particularly when unable to avoid overhanging tea-tree branches. Unlike crack willows which are brittle and will usually break off on impact, these did not give and, if unfortunate enough to get caught up in them, you usually capsized. Flea, positioned on the bow like a figurehead, would anticipate the worst and leap onto the nearest branch and clamber towards the bank just before impact. Weston's final act was to hurl his box camera onto dry land. (Remarkably, it was still working at the end of the trip!) Then began the urgent task of retrieving the apple cases before they sank with all our food and gear.

First lunch stop revealed our mistake in plastering tar over Rose's canoe. After it had been left lying upturned in the sun the tar melted, and you can imagine what happened each time it was manhandled. Tar is not easily removed at the best of times.

In the days when most people owned at least one firearm, and possibly due to the influence of the war, we carried a formidable armoury: three .22 rifles and one .410 shot gun. The latter was the most useful for bowling over rabbits as they hopped along the banks. This required some skill. It was difficult enough to take steady aim while twisted sideways without the added difficulty of having to perform a delicate balancing act in an unstable canoe, so the gun was an ideal weapon under the circumstances. Rabbits were in plague proportions on farms deserted by their owners who had left to serve in the armed forces, so we felt justified in eradicating as many as possible, at the same time allowing us to live off the land.

The day would finish sitting around a camp fire over which was suspended a billy containing an adequate meal of boiled rabbit. Sometimes we would have the luxury of fried fish. Afterwards Weston would entertain us with tunes on his mouth organ. Contented, we would collapse exhausted into sleeping bags, and in spite of the four of us having to squeeze into a two-man tent, immediately fall asleep.

On the wide open stretches of the South Esk we utilised a ground sheet for a sail. Note the apple case seat. Wilson and Weston.

Hawkins, Wilson and Weston at the campsite at Glen Esk bridge. No thought of gun safety!

The end of 1945 saw Weston keen to start again, this time sharing his canoe with Max Wilson, also a rower, and a friend of Weston since primary school days at Lilydale. When he left High School that year Wilson commenced work at the Department of Agriculture, training to become an agronomist under John Tilt who, years later, was to be my father-in-law. He eventually became an agricultural consultant in Perth, Western Australia.

Hawkins managed to convince his father that he could swim sufficiently well to get himself out of trouble and he and I travelled together for the first of many times. We had replaced the hessian covering of my canoe with canvas, which was not quite so easily holed by rocks and snags.

Weston brought along some Dewcrisp dehydrated vegetables and soup mix of onions, potatoes, carrots and peas from the Army Research establishment at Scottsdale. We all thought this was a great idea until we tried them. It didn't pay to be down-wind of anyone after they had partaken of the vegetables or soup mix. A novelty was powdered dried egg which we all agreed tasted little better than sawdust. Another addition was navy life-boat biscuits which were about as digestible as Burnie-board. Apparently these hadn't changed since World War I when my father survived on them after being torpedoed in the Mediterranean.

This trip was memorable for the number of swamp hawks (now called harriers) nesting on the overhanging branches of tea-tree, where we thought their eggs and young would be inaccessible to land predators. We were wrong.

Treachery! Rose and Weston deliberately not warned of tea-tree hazard on the Macquarie River.

Passing close to some nests, Weston suddenly shouted, "Look out! There's a snake near your head." I turned just in time to see a large black reptile eyeing me carefully. We hastily swung the canoe around, and I pulled out the rifle and dispatched it. I would like to add that I did this out of charity for the nestlings, but this would be less than honest. The real reason was to test my marksmanship.

I brought home one of the young birds. At first it didn't like me at all and would peck viciously when I tried to feed it with pieces of rabbit, but eventually we became friends and after being let loose to do its own hunting would return each evening, land in a nearby tree and, when I called, alight on my arm ready to be put back in its cage. I was quite upset when it returned one night and soon died. I could only presume it had picked up some poisoned food.

In the middle reaches of the river, Hawkins and I made a 'faux pas' which we were not allowed to forget. We came to what we thought was a long island. Weston and Wilson followed the main channel and, just to be different, Hawkins and I took what we thought might be a short cut. Progress became more and more difficult the further we went until finally the channel was completely blocked with waterweed and overhanging tea-tree. We had chosen a backwater. While retracing our way the others were pushing ahead thinking we must have succeeded in taking a quicker route. To attract their attention we fired shots into the air but they were too far away to hear us and likewise we couldn't hear them. Thus while we paddled furiously to catch up, they were doing the same. It was nightfall before we finally succeeded in attracting their attention and were able to rejoin them for a late camp.

These balmy summer holidays spent in seeming isolation, lazily drifting over long wide stretches, created a dreamlike state in which we were suspended between sky and water, only waking when the murmuring of a rapid ahead called for action. As the river bottom came up to greet us, red and green ribbons of waterweed wavered in the quickening current. A fish would dart from underneath and disappear in a flash of light. Approaching the drop we peered ahead to see the tell-tale tapering V, indicating the deepest water. Then followed that little thrill of being thrust forward into the next reach.

Ten days after setting off we arrived back at Evandale, having covered what we thought was 150 miles (250 kilometres) in canoes. By now we had run out of mending materials, the canoes were leaking like sieves and more time was spent plastering holes with grass and clay than paddling. Weston resorted to holding a patch over the biggest hole in his canoe with his foot.

One more of these enjoyable adventures down the South Esk, and one from Ross to Longford on the Macquarie River, and we were ready for something more exciting.

The one that never was

In 1946, when Hawkins and I learned it was possible to land a light aircraft on the beach at Lake Pedder, the idea grew that this could be used as a supply depot for crossing southern Tasmania by canoe.

The magnificent beach at the original Lake Pedder, now drowned.

As far as I was concerned, it would have been better to concentrate on my studies. We were both doing first year science at the University of Tasmania, and this was another distraction I could ill afford.

The plan was to ascend the Huon River. From what we could gather it was not a constant torrent but rather a series of pools and rapids. We would paddle and haul the canoes as far upriver as possible, then carry them over the buttongrass plain to Lake Pedder where we could be re-supplied, before descending the Serpentine River which drained the lake into the Gordon River. Then, hopefully, after a few more weeks, we would arrive at Strahan on Macquarie Harbour. We were prepared to spend several months achieving our aim.

We revealed our plan to Ian Grant, a member of the Southern Tasmanian Aero Club. At first he was quite enthusiastic about landing at Lake Pedder but then refused to help when he learned we were to proceed down the Serpentine. He considered the idea suicidal and produced photos to make his point. They showed a river which lived up to its name by meandering in weird contortions over the plain between Lake Pedder and Mt Sprent. Obviously there was little fall and, as it was free of logs, there would be no problem with this stretch. However, from here on the change was dramatic. The Serpentine plunged down between the high hills in an endless cascade of white water to the Gordon.

We had to admit it looked rather daunting, but would still have given it a go. But, no plane, no trip!

In 1954 Olegas Truchanas attempted to get down the same gorge. He lost his canoe and was lucky not to lose his life.

Operation Bungle

Since taking up his teaching post at Queenstown in 1948, Weston often crossed the Franklin, Collingwood and King Rivers, so we asked him to look into the canoeing potential of each. He reported that the King appeared to be the best choice because, as far as he could see, there appeared to be no major hazards and in any case, it was a comparatively short river.

Above: A typical King River campsite among the rocks.
Left: Morning mist in the King River gorge.

Flowing south, between the Eldon Range to the east and the Tyndalls to the west, the Eldon River is joined by the South Eldon to form the King River. Lake Margaret, eight kilometres to the west, has the highest recorded annual average rainfall in Tasmania of 145 inches (3600 mm) per year. With a large catchment area and high rainfall you would expect the river to be subject to flooding. However, this is not how we found it—this year was to be the exception.

Hawkins had examined an aerial survey photograph, one of a series taken by Brown and Dureau after World War II which only covered the length of the river from the Lyell Highway to Crotty. It appeared to be slow flowing with just a few minor rapids.

In the 1940s few people ventured to Tasmania's west. The six hour journey from Launceston to Queenstown was considered a major undertaking.

Hawkins' diary, 15 January, 1949:

"We left in great excitement before a whirring camera in the hands of Wendy Dean—whom Weston, unfortunately, had not shown how to turn off, with the result that, when he ran back to get it, Wendy was desperately filming her family, the house, scenery, hens and anything else she thought might be interesting!!!—she even got a shot of Weston running back, yelling instructions of 'How to turn off movie camera!'. Of this film there is only about half left intact."

[The ensuing quotes in this story are also from Hawkins' diary.]

Ahead lay 160 miles of narrow, winding, mostly gravel road which in some parts was little better than a track. This was particularly so over the last thirty miles from King William Saddle to the King River where blind corners and lack of guard rails made it essential to crawl along. Our 1926 Dodge car cut down to a utility, with poor steering and mediocre brakes, was not the ideal vehicle to transport six people, canoes and all the gear. The driver had to concentrate on the road but the passengers at least had time to gaze in awe at the endless mountains crowding in on each other, their slopes covered in pristine rain forest.

"Weston, Wilson and I sat in the back of the truck till the King River was reached, passing through some very wet weather on the way—our ground sheets merely served to divert the water to the floor of the truck so that we were soon each sitting in our own pool of water."

Weston and Scarlett preparing the folboat for the day's run and tying down the storm cover.

Once past the King River we entered a different world; stark mountains all around almost totally devoid of vegetation. The view from the saddle beyond Gormanston was one of total devastation. The insatiable appetite for wood to fire the furnaces of the Mt Lyell mine at Queenstown, and deadly sulphurous fumes from the copper smelters, had left a barren landscape. The only witness to the former glory of the valley was the occasional blackened stump. Still, we had to admit, there was something fascinating about the weird lunar landscape. Rain heightened the many colours of the mineralised base rock exposed in the road cuttings. We wound our way down the 'ninety-nine' bends to Queenstown.

"With Wilson driving cautiously, Dean, now in the back, promptly nicknamed him L.G. ('Low-Gear') Wilson."

After settling in at the *Caledonian* Hawkins noticed for the first time the absence of a tin containing his movie-camera, films, 3 lbs. of bacon and 2 lbs. of home-made jam! This meant that, although we had Jeff's movie, the only film left was the half Wendy hadn't wasted.

This time the fourth member of the party was Joe Scarlett, who filled in for Max Wilson. Max was able to come along only as a driver to take my vehicle back to Evandale, accompanied by John Hart, an old school friend. We could not have wished for a better replacement than Joe. He and Weston had met while studying for their diplomas in Physical Education at Melbourne University. Joe was powerfully built, yet he was one of the gentlest and kindest people I have ever known. During World War II he had captained an army patrol boat in northern Australian waters.

Weston had an association with this river which must have made him feel slightly uneasy about venturing forth on it. One day in early October 1926 his uncle, William Weston, a pay clerk at Williamsford, perished not far above the (now flooded) King River bridge when caught in a snowstorm while walking from Rosebery to Queenstown.

Our folboats, or fold boats, purchased from army disposals for twenty-five pounds (fifty dollars), were seventeen feet long kayaks. Each wooden skeleton had to be assembled in two halves prior to being forced into a toughened rubberised skin and finally levered into position by one of us standing on a raised hinged section in the middle. The deck was enclosed with canvas tied to the gunwales and a splash cover around our body kept out most of the water when running the rapids. We fitted wide keel boards to protect the folboats' skins from rocks, snags, and abrasions while portaging. Between them the two craft carried over 300 lbs (200 kg) of gear. This included tinned food, cooking utensils, extra paddles, spare woodwork, repair kits, cameras, spare clothing, walking boots, sleeping bags, tent, a .303 rifle, two .22s and a 12 bore shotgun.

You could rightly question our sanity in burdening ourselves with an armoury of this size—we were already overloaded. But these were the days before gun controls when it seemed essential to be armed 'in the bush'.

Also, there was the thought that we could be trapped on the wrong side of a flooded river, run out of food, and have to live off the land. It now seems obvious that travelling lighter would have been more sensible.

The night before departure we camped at the picnic ground below the King River bridge and had not long retired when we had a visit from an animal resembling a black domestic cat but then, in the dying flames of the campfire, we picked out white spots on its body and tail—a tiger cat, or spotted-tailed quoll. I had never seen one before, yet now they are quite common, even in settled areas. The same applied to the rarely seen white cockatoo. We were thrilled to hear and see a pair flying over the gorge a few days later and yet now it is not unusual to find large flocks in farming areas of the Midlands. We had hoped to see or hear a Tasmanian tiger but no such luck.

Max Wilson and John Hart left us with cries of "You'll be sorry." (They weren't far wrong!) We had planned to also 'do' the Pieman River after the King, and return to Evandale via the Emu Bay railway to Burnie and then hitchhike the rest.

The length of river from our starting point to the old smelting works at the abandoned mining town of Crotty was, as we expected, ideal for canoeing. Just before reaching Crotty we passed under the steel railway bridge designed by John Monash for the North Lyell Co., and used briefly for their trains travelling to Kelly Basin on Macquarie Harbour. After the Crotty works closed in 1900 it was used intermittently until 1928.

From Crotty everything changed dramatically—it would be hard to imagine a greater contrast. What the photographs hadn't shown was a forbidding rock-strewn gorge between Mt Huxley to the north and Mt Jukes to the south, the height of both peaks being in the order of 1000 metres. (Charles Gould, the geologist, named the lower peak Huxley after a scientist supporting Darwin's controversial theory of evolution, and the other higher one Jukes, after an opponent to the theory—indicating his own feelings on the subject.)[2]

We now faced a ferocious torrent hurtling down between, or disappearing under huge boulders. Where we could, we 'lined' the unwieldy folboats. One man would hold back upstream with a long rope tied to the stern, while his mate with a rope tied to the bow would go forward to a point from where he could attempt to direct the craft through the best channel. Just before it reached the edge of a big drop the bow man would endeavour to make any final corrections, pulling as hard as he could to prevent the canoe nose-diving and getting stuck on the bottom of the river.

Sometimes things did not go according to plan. The current would take over, sending the canoe on a different course. Then again, we could encounter two or more falls close together, with fast water between.

Even if the stern man succeeded in holding back the canoe there was a good chance it would be swamped, so it was often better for him to let it go, then hurl the rope down towards the bowman and hope he would be able to catch it and hold on. Often the way on your side was barred by huge boulders, or a cliff face, and if your companion was already positioned opposite you would hurl a coiled rope to him so that he could take over while you clambered around the obstacle. The alternative was to paddle furiously to get to the other side before you were swept, broadside on, over the fall.

Weston and Scarlett: a huge log blocking the river created the perfect fall.

Log jams were a hazard. At some time in the past, piners felled logs into the river hoping that floods would carry them down to where they could be caught in a boom across the river mouth and from there be towed over Macquarie Harbour to a sawmill at Strahan. These logs do not rot in water and some remained jammed in the narrow confines of the gorge.

We soon learned to be wary of logs as they seem to draw your craft towards them. Once caught in their deadly embrace there is little you can do to avoid a capsize or damage. The most dangerous situation is to be trapped in a narrow gap. Large rocks change the direction of flow and often, when a collision seems inevitable, the changing current will swing you away from them. Logs obstruct but will not usually deflect your craft.

Averaging no more than a mile a day and our principal food supply down to a few pounds of flour, we were thinking of abandoning the trip when everything was decided for us.

You may wonder why we were short of food after only a few days. In the excitement of departure we left behind the carefully soldered tins of wheatmeal biscuits, our staple diet. If Weston hadn't shot a wallaby (with a .303 army rifle) we would have been forced to abandon the trip earlier. The other disaster was that somehow we managed to get nearly all of our matches wet. The only alternative was to cut the meat into thin steaks and grill these on sticks after warming them on the hot rocks. As this was now our staple diet we couldn't afford to throw any away, and several days of humid weather did nothing to improve the meat's quality. These same rocks also cooked our bare feet, in spite of the trouble we had gone to harden them, by going barefoot as much as possible in the weeks before we left.

Finding campsites amongst the huge boulders was a problem and sometimes we would have to use our tin plates to scoop up sand to make something like a level platform to lie on. It was usually impossible to pitch the tent so all we could do was string it between boulders and hope it wouldn't rain. I don't know what would have happened if the river had risen.

Scarlett and Hawkins with the folboat after it had jammed under a waterfall.

I have mentioned the importance of keeping the bow line taut when lining over a big drop. Once, while acting as bowman, I endeavoured to keep ahead of the kayak which was being pushed along by a fast current but was thwarted by a huge boulder. By the time I managed to clamber over this boulder the craft had passed me and I could do nothing further to direct it. When the rope came to an end I had to let go. At this late stage it was futile for Hawkins, the stern man, to hold back so he had no alternative but to let the rope slide through his hands and hope there would be enough left for him to hold onto after the craft had nosedived over the fall.

The bow wedged itself between rocks on the bottom and there it remained, jammed between the top and bottom of the fall, completely covered by the tumbling water. There was no hope of getting near it, so we could only pull downstream with the remaining rope and hope that the kayak would do a backflip and break free. Not surprisingly the framework collapsed under the strain and the craft buckled and folded over before we were able to pull it away. All we retrieved was a wreck which was dismantled in a backwater.

"We had lunch with quite a bit of chaff and wise-cracking to keep Dean cheerful, but he took it well and, always the newshound, proceeded to photograph the remains."

We salvaged what we could and packed the remains into Weston's craft and struggled on for another mile or so, but progress was too slow for starving men. It was time to walk out.

We headed north. It was a hot, windless day. The vegetation on the sides of the gorge had recently been burnt and the blackened ground absorbed the heat, adding to our misery as we clambered up the steep slopes of Mt Huxley (3,400 feet).

"We struck an old track which, although providing easy walking, led us off course and almost to the King Bend. We looped back, lost the track in a creek bed, climbed out of the gully through dead timber again and decided to make camp at the first good spot. This we did, sleeping on a bed of cut, green branches, although a wet night and a damp bag (our sleeping bags were in the canoes at the time of the swamping) kept me awake for some of the night."

Two days later we emerged at Lynchford, the old Abt railway siding, famished and exhausted. We tried to stop a rail car loading milk for Strahan but the driver merely waved back and went on. Rather annoyed, we went to the nearest home and asked for train information. We found that no trains were running that day so we walked to Queenstown. Here Scarlett had to leave us as his allotted time had run out.

We needed advice about an easier route back to our kayaks, so we made for the Police Station. In spite of our down-and-out appearance the police were very helpful, even allowing us to sleep on the premises. Sergeant Cole, soon christened King Cole, who knew the area well, advised us to return via Harris' Reward track. This wound its way from Lynchford to the old gold diggings on the southern side of the gorge and crossed the King via a suspension bridge a few miles downstream from where we had left our kayaks.

The river widened beyond the bridge into a basin before passing through a second gorge called Dubbil Barril, and King Cole encouragingly informed us that this was a good place to look for bodies swept downstream.

The first part of the corduroy track was quite good. It had been used in the early days by miners with pack horses. However, about a mile after crossing the river it petered out, and we had to scramble over rotting logs and over and under horizontal scrub.

> *"Some time was spent looking for a logging track seen from the other side of the river when walking out, but when found this proved to be steep and overgrown. A quick descent and a search for a camping spot forced us to finally select a damp piece of semi-flat ground perched high on the side of the cliff face. After diverting a stream with rocks and mud we spent a comfortable night sleeping on cut brush and fern fronds to prevent us sinking into mud, but mosquitoes earned the place the name of 'Mosquitoes Reward' from Dean."*

We finally located the spot where we had left the gear back on the other side of the river. I can't remember how we crossed over, but we did. We packed all we could inside Weston's kayak, tied the carry bag containing the salvaged skin and other parts of my folboat on top and proceeded downriver to the old suspension bridge we had used two days earlier. Hawkins wrote a detailed account of subsequent events:

> *"At one spot Dean slipped and fell, fully clothed, into a rapid while lining Weston's kayak and he performed no small feat in reaching a rock at the edge of a 6–7 foot drop and dragging himself onto it. We rescued him by lowering him on the end of the rope onto the canoe and then dragging them both to shore.*
>
> *Then within 1/4 mile of camp Dean, still in wet clothes, went ahead to get tea while Weston and I effected repairs to his kayak—which proved rather extensive, and eventually we incorporated pieces of Dean's wreck into her make-up, notably the stern section.*
>
> *Packing the extra gear into the remaining kayak was a bit of a problem as she was now loaded to the gunwales ... I climbed on ahead as we had decided that two could handle the craft as well as three and, in any case, it was almost impossible for all [of us] to travel on board except in the smoother water ... In calm water two paddled while straddling the kayak with legs dangling in the water ... for the most part we lined the craft as it plunged deeply into the rapids and reappeared all too slowly ... I left with tent and camping gear in the*

EXPENSES of the KING RIVER TRIP.

	£.	s.	d.
Supplies taken with us	3	5	0
Powdered Egg (2 tins)		15	0
Ammunition			
12 bore - 1 box		11	0
.22 bore - 5 boxes		17	6
Spare Stores (dehydrated vegetables, flour, sugar, etc.)		17	0
Stores later bought at Queenstown	1	6	0
Pictures and Suppers		12	0
Board at Queenstown (4 of us)	3	12	0
Petrol	2	2	0
Emu Bay train fare (3 of us) @ 30/-	4	10	0
Queenstown to Zeehan 4/- each		12	0
" " " Canoes		8	0
Total	£18	15	6
or	£ 4	13	6 each

This trip is by far the most expensive we have done -
normally we have paid approximately 30/- each per fortnight.
The extra expense was due to the under-estimated time for
the trip, the fact that we were forced to board in Queenstown and also the cost of the petrol (up till now we have
always been able to reach our rivers by rail)

-----oOo-----

_Hawkins kept the accounts for the King River trip. The cost of the King River trip was equivalent
to $9.35 each, including movies and boarding house in Queenstown._

hope of making camp at the bridge while the others caught up and although expecting the bridge to appear after rounding each bend, I was never rewarded. In fact on several occasions I was presented with a view of almost vertical cliffs often made slippery and wet with moss and small water courses.

It must have been a lucky day for me for on at least three occasions I was forced to hang literally by toes and finger tips, and three times said a very short prayer, and fully expected that Mrs Hawkins' little boy would fail to answer the breakfast gong in the morning. For some reason I took risks that would normally appal me—however, in spite of the cumbersome rucksack, I did live to tell the tale.

Once, when halfway up a cliff face, I found my hold tearing loose, and seeing a gum tree growing from the side some distance below me, I jumped for its branches—it swayed a lot and swung out further from the cliff but held, and so I was able to slither down its trunk and after a further descent reached the river's edge again.

Rounding what I thought to be a final corner, I was disappointed in not seeing the bridge and, so crossing a fairly respectable camping site

Above: The three bushrangers, Scarlett, Weston and Hawkins, after a two-day walk out on reduced rations.

amongst driftwood, I decided to make use of it. I had barely got a fire going and billy on, and commenced putting up the tent, when the others arrived cursing a difficult portage which they apparently had to perform. A hurried tea but sufficient with everybody keen to get to bed—and that's where I'm off to now.

Thursday—A beautiful day and, with the river having dropped a foot during the night, Jeff [Weston] and self lined the canoe around three bends and the bridge hove in sight. A log halted operations for a while, (we came across several of these logs—usually Huon pine—enormous things jammed across the full width of the river and about 3–4 feet through and which had probably been there since very early days and so would now be worth a small fortune) but finally, we unloaded and beached the canoe and dismantled her.

Dean then commenced salvage operations on 'Glider' by committing all damaged woodwork to the executioner's axe—and only the brass fittings (and skin) being saved, and with Weston's added wreckage we carried out a short cremation ceremony with heads bowed in memory of 'Glider'! However, she made good firewood and served to boil a brew in record time. We lunched on the stores left under the bridge, in very hot conditions and myself feeling practically par-boiled."

Here we cut some poles from the bush with a machete, suspended the packaged folboats from these and, shouldering the loads like porters carrying big game, set off on the four mile (6 km) slog to Lynchford Railway Siding. I was in the lead when a tiger snake reared up in front and refused to give way. Handicapped as I was by the heavy load, I was in no position to argue so I gave in and stepped around it; I don't like snakes at the best of times.

Returning with a second load we barely had time to collapse on the platform of the railway station at Lynchford before an engine belching white smoke appeared down the line. This was the annual picnic train, its open trucks covered with awnings, crammed tight with Mt Lyell workers and their families returning from a day by the sea at Strahan. We wondered first of all if the driver would stop and, second, if there was room for us and our gear. No need to worry. With the typical generosity of West Coast people they helped us aboard and somehow managed to squeeze us in. The whistle blew and we were on our way to Queenstown.

After catching the bus to Zeehan, we boarded the Emu Bay Railway train, and headed for Burnie. On the way we were delighted with a view of the Pieman River and its canoeing prospects. This led to a discussion about building more suitable canoes which occupied us for the rest of the four hour journey.

"We arrived at Devonport at about 11.30 pm … and I ran ahead to find the Police Station in the hope of being able to sleep in the Court-house as at Queenstown. However, the cop proved very unhelpful and,

I think, felt more than half inclined to run me in—he may have had some reason as I had entered his office, unshaven for a fortnight, and carrying a gun at 12 o'clock midnight in a town full of Saturday night drunks and shore-leave sailors, with a wild tale of having canoed the King River (which is, by the way, something like 100 miles from Devonport). Luckily, the others arrived and rescued me but, eventually, we slept in an unlocked guards van in the goods yard … courtesy of the Tasmanian Government Railways—so ending, as John Dean named it, 'Operation Bungle'.

After all our efforts we covered only about 30 miles of the river (normally one day's good paddle!) and of this distance the first 7 miles had been done in less than a day—a fortnight had been spent in covering the remaining distance."

In Hawkins' words, *"I thought it was nearer to being a mountaineering expedition [than a canoe trip], with canoes taken along as extra gear."* We had no thoughts of returning to the King River.

Above: Two exhausted members of the party, Weston (left) and Hawkins, waiting at Lynchford Station for the Abt railway train.

Left: The picnic train arrives. Note the canvas awnings covering trucks packed with picnickers. Somehow we managed to squeeze on board.

CHAPTER 4
PIEMAN RIVER—1950

Rumble in the jungle

The King River fiasco should have been enough to deter any sane person from ever attempting anything like it again. But youthful enthusiasm prevailed and towards the end of 1950 we commenced feverish preparations for an attempt to canoe an even lesser-known river, the Pieman.

Above left: Wilson, Weston, Hawkins.
Above right: A scene from Hawkins' 9.5 mm Pathe movie film. Wilson and Weston.

Why was such a beautiful river inflicted with such a weird name? The most popular explanation is its association with the convict "Jimmy the Pieman", who was captured on the banks of the river after escaping from the Sarah Island penal settlement in Macquarie Harbour.[3]

The first exploration of the Pieman was by Lieutenant James Hobbs of the Royal Navy during the autumn of 1824, in a small rowing boat manned by convicts. He succeeded in getting up-river almost as far as the dolerite gorge.[4] Fifty years elapsed before prospectors came to nearby Heemskirk searching for tin.

The confluence of the Mackintosh and Murchison rivers near Tullah once marked the beginning of the old Pieman (before it was inundated by waters backing up from the Reece Dam in 1987). The much enlarged river is joined by six major tributaries draining a huge area to its north. A 1:250000 map showed us a river dropping a modest 300 feet (roughly 100 metres) in the 60 miles (100 km) between Rosebery, just below our starting point, and Corinna on the estuary where we hoped to finish.

This didn't seem too much of a worry until Miss Thirkell of *Fern Hill*, Nile, volunteered some information which gave me something to think about. Her father, R.A.C. Thirkell, who had been involved with exploration of the west coast, once told her there was a huge waterfall on the Pieman and she warned me to be very careful not to get swept over it.

Much later I read that he was quite prominent as an explorer in other areas in the west around the turn of the century. In 1900 he was a member of T.B. Moore's party which cut a track from Macquarie Harbour to Port Davey. They nearly perished after their stores there were pilfered and they had to return by the same route to survive. In 1907 Thirkell was in charge of a party which at first followed J.L.A. Moore's track from the Linda Track to the Jane River–Acheron junction before continuing on towards the Gordon.[5]

Getting to the upper Pieman fifty years ago was an interesting experience. With no road, the only access was by the Emu Bay Railway. It was raining when we arrived at Guildford Junction, 45 miles (75 km) south of Burnie. The train was not leaving for Zeehan until the next day and we were allowed to spend the night in the Ladies' Waiting Room. Enquiries revealed that the best starting point would be just before reaching the Pieman Bridge, two miles north of Rosebery, where rail and river came close together and the train would make an unscheduled stop for us to unload our folboats. The fact that we were still using

Opposite: The dolerite cliff face of the Pieman gorge.

Right: Dean (only the pith helmet visible) and Hawkins.

these shows that we hadn't entirely lost faith in them and at this time there was nothing better available.

The members of the party were the same as for the King River disaster except that, unfortunately, Joe Scarlett was unable to be with us this time. He had been a pillar of strength during the King ordeal. His place was taken by Max Wilson, who had been with us in '44 and '46 on the South Esk. He was not quite as mad as the rest of us and only agreed to come along under sufferance. After the main food supply had been left behind last time, Hawkins took things into his own hands and organised the rations. His enthusiasm was growing with each trip.

My diary:

"Thursday Dec. 28, 1950. Spent the day assembling folboats, swimming and packing gear. Ideal weather and prospects are for an exciting day tomorrow. We are prepared for tip-ups. Weston as usual enjoying some fishing and has been digging for worms. Camped about 50 feet above water on sandy ledge. The atmosphere smells of rain.

Next day. Finally embarked about midday in rain after waiting for weather to clear. According to gauge near the bridge river is below summer level. Weston and Wilson capsized later in day and wet most of their (spare) clothes and our sleeping bags. We camped about the same height above the water on a mossy bank. Weston caught two small fish and four eels.

Saturday. Rained till late morning. Departed about 11 am. Lunched on rock shoal in warm sun. Very nearly swamped under projecting log in rapid. Hawkins (in stern) had to abandon ship and it then broke free. We managed to shoot all rapids, bottoming on a few. Again there were periodic showers. The scenery has been magnificent.

Sunday. Awakened at 6 am after a restless night by Wilson banging on a billy. Away by 9 am and covered about 14 miles today. We lunched once more on a rocky shoal. There is an abundance of these. We holed on a rock in one of the many rapids. This was the only mishap of the day. The river has widened since the entry of the Wilson and Stanley Rivers (we think). We camped on a high bank again, below the latter. If we are correct in our assumptions progress has surpassed expectations. We bagged five fish by trailing spinners.

Right: Wilson.

*Monday, 1 Jan. 1951. New Year's Day and no resolutions. Left at
10 am—late start after patching kayak. We passed through more rapids
than any other day and two or three were of King River proportions.
Hawkins filmed us in the rapids with his 9.5 mm Pathe movie camera
and I took my first colour slides. We lunched on a beach between
rapids and amused ourselves by trying to put bullets through tins
thrown in the air. We have reached a point where the river flows
east–west for a few miles. Prospects are for rapids continuing for some
miles. This is written by firelight—mosquitoes troublesome. A high
camp again.*

*Weston has discovered the pine trees growing around the camp are in
fact Huon pines. There are a lot of them, about one foot in diameter.
Also celery-top pines."*

Weston's diary:
*"We have (been) spilling over rapid after rapid without any disasters.
It has been super duper!"*

Then something happened which changed our mood from exhilaration to
foreboding. We were above the main gorge and gliding over a calm stretch of
water when we heard what sounded like distant thunder downriver, but this
didn't make sense because it was a clear day with no thunderclouds. My next
thought was that it might be waves crashing against a rocky shore. Then I
realised that the sea was
some thirty miles away.
There could only be one
explanation. It must be

*Above: Muscle man.
The author in his prime.*

Left: Dean and Hawkins.

29

the treacherous waterfall Miss Thirkell had warned about, and it made me uneasy. What if we came upon it unexpectedly and couldn't stop? But then all my attention was given to negotiating the demanding rapids of the dolerite gorge and I forgot about it. After that we didn't hear the rumble again. We concluded the mysterious sound must have been carried upstream from the rapids. We were wrong. The mystery was not solved until fourteen years later when, with another party of canoeists, we found the real cause of the ominous boom.

My diary again:

"Tuesday. Weston and I inspected a group of Huon pines near camp before leaving. Some of these are up to three feet (one metre) in diameter. By lunch (on smooth rocks) we had cleared the last of the rapids in the gorge. Thus it took a full day to get through the gorge proper. Often more by good luck than good management we escaped tip-ups. Once we got stuck on a rock, at the head of some fast water, and after several minutes broke free to blunder through the remainder of the fall.

Between lunch and camp we passed over long, wide stretches with occasional minor rapids. We trolled for fish, but only Weston managed to get two small ones. We travelled east–west for several miles, then north-east, south and west each for about a mile, then several miles north. We covered about 12 miles (20 km). Tomorrow we travel NNE. We spent some time photographing each other in rapids.

There are two fine myrtle beeches and a blackwood within a few feet of the tent, once more at a height about 30 feet (10 m) above the water. Apparently these ledges are at flood level. It is the only flat ground.

We estimate the distance to Corinna to be about 30 miles (50 km) so we should arrive the day after tomorrow, provided the map is reliable.

Above: I took my first colour slides on this trip. Wilson and Weston (above); Dean and Hawkins (below).

Opposite: Wilson.

Wednesday, 3 Jan. 1951. It's over! The distance from last camp to Corinna was ten miles (16 km) short of what we estimated. Our first surprise came when we saw a sign "Pieman Rapids". This was beside a bushfire warning notice. We remained puzzled until two miles further on we came to another sign marking the Paradise River. We knew then we were in the home stretch."

Near the Paradise River we encountered four men fishing from a dinghy. We were surprised to be told they were expecting us. Apparently when we set out someone had given a report of our proposed trip to *The Advocate*, the north-west Tasmanian newspaper. The story was that we were going to live off the land. (I suppose they assumed we had enough armaments for this anyway!) Consequently these fisherman, all from Devonport, thought we must be starving and kindly offered us a tin of cakes, followed later by some fish. If only these good Samaritans had appeared on our previous King River trip! This time, for a change, our food supplies were plentiful.

We were fortunate to be able to get a hut to sleep in that night, for after a week of almost perfect weather more normal conditions returned and the downpour would have made life a misery in our barely adequate tent.

The minor inconveniences experienced on the Pieman were trivial compared to the hardships we had suffered on the King, and yet, considering this river was more remote and to the best of our knowledge had never been explored over its full length, we couldn't get over our good fortune at having

The billy boils at one of the delightful campsites on the flood ledges amongst the Pieman River rainforest.

so little trouble canoeing it for the first time. Even so, we were lucky to have ideal conditions for negotiating the grade three rapids in the dolerite gorge, which I found later could be far more demanding when the river level was higher.

The journey home this time was not without incident. First of all, Weston had to get a lift from Corinna back to Guildford Junction where he had left the old Dodge utility. Alleston Gray, a lady from Launceston, was going as far as Waratah, but kindly took him further on to Guildford. He arrived back in the evening so we agreed to spend another night in the hut.

Soon after we left next morning the road deteriorated into potholes and corrugations so Weston decided to drive on the wrong side of the road, claiming that it was less rough that way. All went well until he met a car on a blind corner and had to take evasive action to avoid a head-on collision. He succeeded brilliantly in missing the other car but in so doing ran out of road and ploughed into the left bank, bending back the front axle.

To partially compensate for this we loosened off the elliptical main spring U-bolts and moved the axle forward and after that proceeded cautiously with a wheel very much out of alignment. This worked for a while and then the strain on the axle proved too much and the wheel folded over to a grotesque angle.

There was nothing else for it but to remove the axle and get it straightened. This involved hitching a ride to Burnie, an overnight stay, and then getting a blacksmith to heat and straighten it. (For a cost of ten shillings—one dollar!)

By the time we arrived back to the buttongrass plain where the vehicle was jacked up, darkness was closing in and rain was bucketing down. Hawkins and Wilson had hitched a ride earlier in the day. Weston and I spent a miserable night camped in the back of the ute with a barely waterproof tent covering us.

Instead of one day to get home it took three.

Right: Our transport after the accident. The owner Weston, Hawkins and Wilson.

POSTSCRIPT

The Pieman's appeal never left me, so I was keen to go back and show it to my new wife, Stephanie, on our honeymoon. We drove to Guildford Junction through the beautiful rainforest of Hellyer Gorge and arrived just in time to hurl our folded canoe and all our supplies into the guard's van, get tickets for Zeehan and, with beating hearts, clamber aboard the departing train.

Unlike the 1951–52 expedition when we had pitched our tent on a sandbank close to the river, this time we had the use of a new hut right beside the railway line. One drawback was that during the night, as northbound trains came off the bridge and rounded a bend, their powerful light shone straight into the hut, nearly blinding us, and when we were half asleep the thundering engine seemed to be heading directly for us.

Rain set in and the temperature plummeted. This should have been expected; it was early April. After blocking a broken window pane with a copy of *The Examiner* newspaper (featuring our wedding photo) we eventually managed to get a fire going. Wood, especially dry wood, was scarce, but we were not concerned as we planned to proceed down the river next day. This was not to be. According to the gauge near the railway bridge, the river had risen nineteen feet (6 metres) overnight, and there was no indication that it would stop. But for the kindness of the engine driver we would have have suffered a miserable existence. As the train drew level he would throw off a large shovelful of coal towards the door of the hut.

It was still raining after four days. We decided our fragile craft, a lightly constructed collapsible kayak, was not adequate to handle the swirling waters. We stopped the next goods train and requested that our VW be sent on to Zeehan, and saw it go past later that day. The following morning the passenger train stopped for us and we too were on our way. Where else would you get service like that?

Above: Huon pine (Lagarostrobus franklinii).
Opposite: The Pieman rainforest.

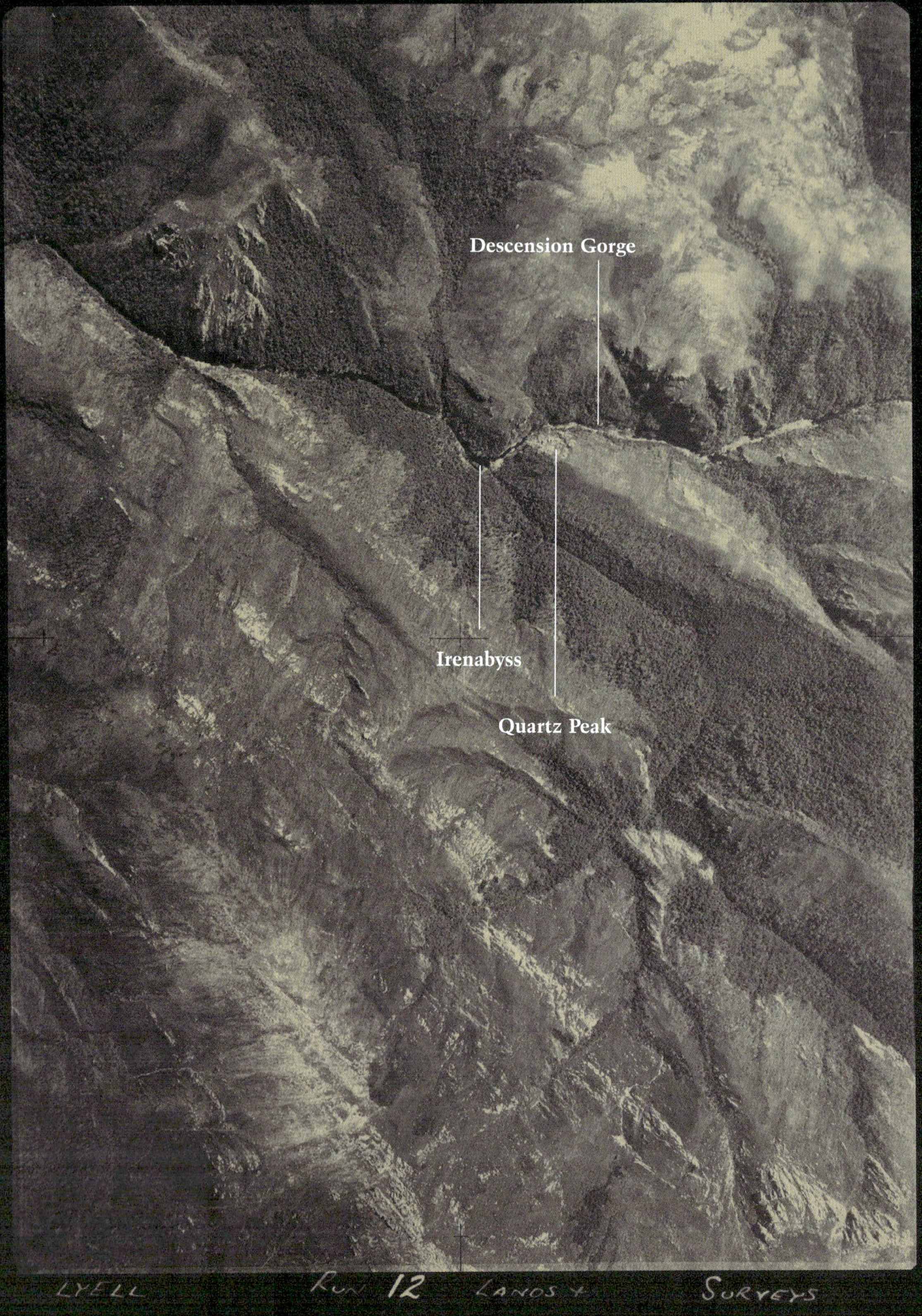

Descension Gorge

Irenabyss

Quartz Peak

LYELL RUN 12 LANDS + SURVEYS

First encounter

After the successful Pieman expedition we regained sufficient confidence to look further afield. Memories of the King River fiasco faded and another partly unexplored river captured our imagination.

Above: Monospar VH-UTH (the only one left, now at the Newark Air Museum, England), used by us in 1950 to reconnoitre the river before our canoeing attempt. We were later told that if one engine failed we would be lucky to maintain height.
Opposite: Aerial photographs helped us plan our trip.

Why had the Franklin never been canoed? It could be easily accessed from the Lyell Highway, even if there it was rather shallow. An even easier entry, from the same highway, could be via the Collingwood, a tributary of the Franklin. This should save about one day's travel because of the shorter distance and deeper water. At journey's end, it would not be a problem to meet up with the tourist launch from Strahan on the lower Gordon, into which the Franklin, in turn, flowed.

However, we soon realised that getting to and from the river was the easy part. Once on the river we would have to cover 60 miles (100 km) and, more significantly, descend 1000 feet (300 metres). Previous experience showed that distance was not as important as the amount of fall in estimating the time it takes to canoe a river. A rough guide was that we averaged a drop of about 75 feet (20 metres) per day. In that case it would take at least 14 days to make the journey, disallowing the time taken to portage around major obstacles, such as waterfalls or log jams. In an area where the average rainfall was 120 inches (over 3000 mm) per year there was a good chance we would be delayed by floods. If all this was not enough, then the warnings from those who purported to know the area should have deterred us.

Aerial view of the Livingston/Franklin River junction in the Great Ravine. The Livingston Rivulet is on the left, hidden by overhanging cliffs. The Coruscades rapids (right) are below Hawkins Blaze (foreground). This photograph was taken in 1959.

In 1850 Tasmanian historian and newspaper editor, John West, wrote that where the "vile" waters of the Franklin and Gordon rivers entered the sea "the fish ... rise up in the waves and float poisoned to the shores." [6]

Marcus Clarke took up the theme in 1874:

"The Gordon ... being fed by numerous rivulets, which ooze through masses of decaying vegetable matter, is of so poisonous a nature that is not only undrinkable, but absolutely kills the fish, which in stormy weather are driven in from the sea. The air is chill and moist, the soil prolific only in prickly undergrowth and noxious weeds, while foetid exhalations from swamp and fen cling close to the humid, spongy ground." [7]

In 1840 when James Calder attempted to find a route for a road to connect the settled areas of eastern Tasmania with Macquarie Harbour, the purpose being to avoid a treacherous sea route, he discovered and named the Franklin, after Sir John Franklin, Governor of Van Diemen's Land. (Sir John was later lost attempting to discover the North-West Passage between the Atlantic and Pacific Oceans.) Calder's description of the Great Ravine was not reassuring:

"I tried to lead the road across at several points but was thwarted by the intervention of a tremendous ravine. I twice got to the bottom of this hideous defile but was at last forced to relinquish the idea of a direct course, and retraced my steps to Lachlan Plains, utterly disgusted with the adventure." [8]

One hundred years after Calder's epic journey the three Morrison brothers from Strahan hauled their punt *upstream* as far as Mt Fincham. [9] It seems the reason for doing it the hard way was that they had been warned, if they attempted to go downstream, they would almost certainly be swept over a waterfall, one hundred feet high! But we didn't know anything about their experiences. If we had, we could have obtained some first hand information and been in a better position to understand what we were up against. What little we had heard so far was not encouraging. It seemed prudent to take a look ourselves.

On a clear spring morning in 1950 Hawkins and I took off from Western Junction airport in a 1930s vintage twin engined Monospar, piloted by Max Kitto of Launceston. We climbed over the Western Tiers and were soon over the "land of a thousand lakes" and finally majestic Lake St Clair surrounded by its guardian peaks. Maintaining a south-west course we passed between Mt Hugel and Mt Rufus. In between we thought we identified Lake Undine, near the source of the Franklin. This lake is filled by water flowing from the Cheyne Range. Soon after we spied a larger Franklin where it met the Lyell Highway. It must have been in flood because the perception was that of a continuous cascade of white water, too rough to even consider tackling. (Years later our family rafted this stretch when the water was low, and found it to be quite friendly.) The river widened after its confluence with the larger Collingwood.

What next impressed us was a long gorge which didn't look at all inviting. This is now called Descension Gorge. Its rushing water exited through a narrow chasm. Unfortunately, we could not make out what lay between the cliffs. Later on, this proved to be a costly gap in our knowledge. If Descension Gorge was frightening, then Deception Gorge (the Great Ravine) was terrifying. Some of the fiercest rapids were bordered by sheer cliffs, making lining or portaging almost impossible or extremely hazardous. By now we were flying well below the tops of the peaks, 600 metres above the Franklin, banking and turning in order to follow the river, reassured by the boom of the two engines echoing from the hillsides. Fifty years later I recounted this to another Aero Club pilot, Lindsay Millar. He was horrified. "If one engine had failed you would have been lucky to maintain a long glide!"

After a safe return we compared our impressions and agreed that this was going to be a tough nut to crack. So much depended on the weather. With a flooded river the gorges would not be good places to be stranded. If forced to abandon the attempt we would be faced with many days of strenuous walking over some of Tasmania's roughest country.

On the afternoon of December 28, 1951, we launched our folboats and set off down the Collingwood. The members of the party were the same as for the King debacle: Weston, Scarlett, Hawkins and I. The river was high and fast. In late January and February water levels are more stable and it would have been preferable to go then, but with holiday constraints we could not choose the ideal time. Hawkins and I capsized in the first rapid and lost a paddle and a boot. After this we tied *everything* in. We portaged around numerous logs and the biggest of the rapids and, making slow progress, covered a mere two miles that afternoon, not even getting as far as the Franklin junction.

For the next three days, progress continued to be slow and hazardous. Sometimes the more innocuous looking rapids are deceptively dangerous, as we were to find out. We managed to get caught in a 'stopper'. A stopper is a concentrated flow of water falling over a drop into comparatively still water which creates a surface back flow, drawing you back under the falling water. To help prevent this happening you build up enough speed to keep moving after plunging over the fall. The worst situation is to go over sideways. Then you have no momentum to carry you away and the effect of the reverse flow is exacerbated. The best you can hope to do is push yourself away with your paddle. If this fails the canoe rapidly fills, becomes unstable and, with water pushing down more on one side than the other, capsizes. The danger then is that it will keep rolling, and extricating yourself is very difficult. To avoid drowning you must escape as quickly as possible and, once free, drop well below the surface to use the reverse flow to carry you downstream.

This time we were lucky in getting away with a water-filled kayak, but before we could get ashore to empty it we were swept into the next rapid, hit rocks, and broke several of the five-foot (1.5 m) lengths of dowelling. These were replaced with spares but in future we would have to cut new ones from saplings in the bush.

We revelled in shooting some excellent rapids. The weather had improved to the extent that we could discard most of our clothing and keep it more or less dry. Then at the end of the fourth day rain set in. The usual cry went up: *"Il pleut, il pleut"* (It's raining, it's raining), more to make light of our forebodings than anything else. In expectation of a flood we took the precaution of camping forty feet up from the river. With such large catchments and vast tributaries these west coast rivers can rise quickly after only a small amount of rain.

Next morning we anxiously peered through the mist to gauge the state of the river. It had risen about two metres and the rushing torrent showed no sign of slowing. It would be difficult or impossible to stop if you had to scout ahead. We decided to stay put.

January 2, 1952. A day to remember. Conditions were no better than the previous day, the river was still in flood and weather prospects were not good. We should have remained in camp.

The minor rapids had been ironed out but the larger ones were more formidable than ever. Between these, whirlpools threatened disaster. The wild swings of the current threw us off balance and each time my kayak lurched to one side my heart was in my mouth in case it didn't right itself. What was even more ominous was the sight of a log being sucked down the vortex of a whirlpool.

Before we entered Descension Gorge proper the river narrowed and passed between high cliffs. Suddenly the ravine filled with the guttural calls of dozens of great black cormorants as they left their nests on the rocky ledges and flew off in alarm. We gazed at the rookery for a few moments and then decided to take some eggs to see if they were edible. Even shag eggs might prove a welcome change of diet in the arduous days ahead. There was no bank on which to land. Hawkins held the canoe under a projecting rock spur while I climbed up to the first nests. The eggs I carried down Hawkins later described as "rough-looking things, as though cast in plaster-of-Paris". Anyway, we took some with us but never had a chance to taste them for disaster overtook us within half a mile.

When we couldn't see the bottom of a fall or around a bend it was often necessary to land and scout ahead. In order to save time, the first ones away would go ahead and only stop when it seemed necessary to go ashore to take a good look at a potentially life-threatening situation. When the others caught up they would be advised to either proceed while still looking out for certain hazards, or stop to line the craft or, worse still, prepare for a portage. If you were lucky enough to be told to keep going, then it was your turn to stop at the next major hazard. Hawkins called this technique 'leap frogging'.

Scarlett and Weston headed off into the gorge first. After a short distance we caught up, and as we swept past called out to them, "What's ahead?"

"Shoot the first two, then stop before the bend," seemed to be the gist of what they shouted above the noise of the rapids. Whatever the message was it didn't make any difference. We couldn't stop, and were soon caught by a raging torrent and carried relentlessly on; on into a forbidding high walled gorge with endless rapids extending into the mist beyond. We would have to ride this one out. Now committed, survival was the most important thing.

First indications were that we might succeed. Coordination was good and we managed to point the craft in the right direction, even with decisions made at the last moment. Then suddenly danger loomed ahead. Jutting out from the bank was a large flat rock barring our way. We reacted by furiously paddling to keep moving faster than the current so that we could keep control and endeavour to manoeuvre the cumbersome craft around the obstruction. When we realised we were not going to manage this, the only thing left to do was backpaddle for all our worth to lessen the impact.

We hit hard.

The bow rose skyward, and for a moment we remained held by the fierce current. Then, with water pouring in, we slipped backwards, the current took hold and whipped us around. We capsized and were thrown out. Emerging on opposite sides of the upturned vessel, we tried desperately to cling to it—our life support—as long as possible, but there was nothing suitable to hang on to and, after plunging over a big drop, the canoe nosedived and jammed, and we were swept away from it.

Surfacing, I anxiously looked around for Hawkins. He was nowhere to be seen. If there was any chance of sighting him I had to get ashore without delay. I don't know how far I was swept downstream before being able to take advantage of a lull in the current, strike out for the 'bank' and claw my way up onto a slippery rock from where I hoped to get a better view of the gorge. From there I sighted Hawkins floating downstream, head first, his face up and supported by his Mae West, so I was not too concerned. What puzzled me was that he looked relaxed, something not to be expected under the circumstances, and was not making any effort to save himself. I can't remember shouting out to him but certainly I thought, "Why the hell don't you try to get out?" Then it hit me; he must be unconscious. I had to get to him as quickly as possible.

I raced downriver hopping from rock to rock and where this wasn't possible plunging across pools, until I was finally baulked by a cliff about thirty metres high rising sheer from the water. I had to climb up and over in order to continue down river. From the top there was a good view of the seemingly endless gorge. No sign of Hawkins. Now I began to believe I would never see him again. How could an unconscious man survive this wild water? Feeling sick at heart, I nevertheless felt impelled to continue searching on the slim chance I would find him.

Quartz Peak, photographed during the 1958 trip. Dean climbed over the peak in 1951 and brought Hawkins back. Both climbed it again in 1958 to bypass the still unknown Irenabyss.

In order to get further downstream I had to climb much higher up an escarpment of loose quartz rock in the hope that beyond this peak there might be calmer water. The higher I climbed the steeper it became until it seemed impossible to continue. But then the thought of descending was even more daunting: one slip and I would hurtle down hundreds of metres into the roaring gorge. Searching around for a way, I spied an angled depression. I edged myself over to it and just managed to get a handhold and clamber past the top of the peak. I raced down a ridge which took me to a vantage point overlooking a backwater. If Hawkins hadn't been swept into this then there was little hope for him. What a relief when I spotted a figure lying on his back on a low rock. His legs were still in water but his head and shoulders were clear. This looked hopeful.

I had to know whether he was still alive so I yelled out, "Are you all right?" which now sounds rather silly because obviously he was not. Imagine my relief when after a few moments I received back a barely audible "Yes".

Hawkins recalled:

"In the following moments I lived a lifetime ... I experienced the terrifying sensation of being swept over a succession of waterfalls ... I learned that the most dangerous part of it is the turmoil under the foot of each fall where you are held under by the weight of the falling water, that unless you can kick bottom and extricate yourself, you cartwheel until you drown ... It's a nightmare, I thought, as I was swept down river.

I could just see things going past me ... the walls of the gorge, jutting rocks, boulders ... I was going straight for a rock ... I was going to hit it ... then I was past it and another rock loomed up in my way. Once I was hurled on to a rock and for a split second I clung on to it like a spider, then I was swept downriver again. It didn't seem possible that I could be alive. The whole thing was a horror but—I kept thinking—if I hit a rock then I'll wake up ... then I'll be back in reality.

I must have lost consciousness because my next recollections are of bobbing down a current free of rapids. The gorge, I recall, had narrowed down to a little passage with rock walls rising sheer hundreds of feet on either side. There were no banks, only sheer rock. Then the gorge blossomed out to a quiet pool where friendly eddies washed me ashore where I lay, panting and exhausted, and not believing that I was still alive. A thought hit my mind. I must be the only survivor. If the other canoe had survived I would have seen the wreckage ...

So it was with a strange feeling of relief that I heard a shout, and looking up, saw a battered Dean standing several hundred feet above." [10]

When I got down to where he lay I could see he was not in good shape. He was too weak to drag himself completely out of the water. His clothing was ripped and he was deathly pale. It was a miracle he had survived.

I had no idea what had happened to Weston and Scarlett, so as soon as Hawkins could gather enough strength we struggled back upstream to look for them. We reached the top of the quartz escarpment I had climbed earlier and were able to avoid the perilous descent by keeping to the tops of the buttongrass covered hills for a good distance before making our way down to where we could get a view of the gorge. Luck was with us. We caught sight of our sunken folboat at the bottom of a cliff face and a figure retrieving gear from it, and above him another figure on a ledge holding a rope which was tied to the man below. We were overjoyed to find our companions, who by now were convinced we had not survived. The last thing they expected was to hear our call from above; they thought it was our ghosts! We clambered down. What a joyous reunion. We were all still alive.

While Hawkins and I had been having our share of drama, Weston and Scarlett had not got off scot-free. They had swamped at the beginning of the gorge but managed to swim with their kayak to a rocky backwater.

Descension Gorge, where Hawkins nearly drowned. This photograph was taken looking upstream from Irenabyss at a later date and in more tranquil conditions, but when in flood these rapids are a major hazard.

Weston took out the .303 and fired a few shots to let us know where they were. We didn't hear a thing. Not getting any response they presumed we must have drowned. They began searching for our bodies. This was no easy task. In order to get downstream with their kayak they had to line their craft from rock ledges. From here they spotted our wreck, jammed against boulders at the foot of a precipice with only the bow showing above water. They presumed our bodies were inside. Fixing a rope Scarlett climbed down to investigate. Not finding us he prudently grabbed a haversack containing clothes and sleeping bags. It was then that they heard our call from above.

The first task was to retrieve my kayak and see if it was repairable. Scarlett attached a rope to the bow and we pulled with all our might in an attempt to get it out of the water onto some rocks, but before we could achieve this the attachment to which the rope was tied broke off and the kayak began to drift away. For a few seconds I was tempted to jump in after it but courage failed me. I had been through enough traumas for one day. Besides, it was raining again.

Hawkins' condition deteriorated. He was shivering uncontrollably. We erected the tent on a rocky ledge, got him inside, and helped him into some more or less dry clothes. Remarkably, some of these were the ones that Scarlett had the foresight to rescue from our kayak before it disappeared forever. Then we got him into the driest sleeping bag. We knew we would have difficulty lighting a fire but when we discovered that all our matches were wet, in spite of taking what we thought were adequate precautions to keep them dry, we knew it was hopeless. So after partaking of some cold food we settled in for a miserable night.

Next morning I awoke to the sound of a crackling fire. Scarlett's ingenuity saved the day. During the night he had worked out a solution to our problem. He removed the cordite from a .303 bullet, placed it on a rock in the sun-light, and then, using his reading glasses as a magnifying glass, concentrated the weak sun's rays onto the cordite until it was hot enough to ignite. Then he added some finely crushed dry bark to the flame, followed by wood shavings and progressively larger sticks until there was a blaze big enough to boil the billy. We sat around enjoying the supreme delight of a hot brew and discussed what to do next.

Hawkins was still far from well and must have been suffering from shock and hypothermia. It seemed wise to get him to permanent shelter as soon as possible. We had heard that the Hydro Electric Commission had built a hut near Mt Fincham for their hydrographers to use while recording river flows. We concluded that there must be a track into this which would make our exit much easier, so we set off in search of it.

Weston ferried Hawkins and me across to the northern side. He and Scarlett proceeded down a now more subdued river while we endeavoured to keep up with them by making our way through thick scrub. We reached more lightly timbered country where we thought we could spy out the land. The others were of the same opinion and landed. We all made for the highest hill and scanned the countryside to the west. There was no hut in sight. We decided it was time to walk out regardless.

In searching for a suitable place to cache Weston's kayak we came across an old hut which had probably been used by the piners. This was about twelve metres above the river and seemed a safe place to leave the canoe. We camped for the night. After a hurried breakfast next morning we set off to walk out, heading north.

We left the forbidding gorge with no regrets. The roar of the rapids faded as we climbed higher and higher and we eventually emerged onto open buttongrass, Mary Creek Plain. Here we were greeted by a sight I will not forget. The rays of the early morning sun highlighted an expanse of Christmas bells (*Blandfordia*), their red and yellow blooms brilliant against a background of sombre buttongrass. They seemed to be saying, "Cheer up, life's not so bad after all." It's marvellous what you see when you haven't got a camera! Both Hawkins' and mine were lost with the folboat.

The next day we were treated to a display of another kind. We had reached the top of the Raglan Range and stumbled onto a vehicular timber track heading down the mountainside in the right direction, so on the strength of our good fortune in finding this we decided to take a break. By now Hawkins and I were struggling along just about barefooted. During the drama of losing the folboat we had also lost our three remaining walking boots. These had been carried for an eventuality such as this. Now our footwear was limited to old canoeing sandshoes. These had holes punched in the sides to let the water drain out. They were no match for the sharp quartz rocks we encountered. When it was decided to call a halt we didn't object and used the time to bandage our feet with whatever clothing could be spared.

Then, as if on cue, hundreds of spine-tailed swifts appeared, performing aerobatics as they dived, rose up and dived again, the only noise coming from their beating wings. Meanwhile, above them others circled, apparently awaiting the opportunity to swoop down on unsuspecting insects. We wondered if it were true that these graceful flyers (now called needletails) lived most of their lives on the wing, only coming to earth when they nest in the northern hemisphere. Their flight was so effortless that we thought this possible. There was something ethereal about them.

Weston sensed this. He felt that they were farewelling him.

He never returned to the Franklin.

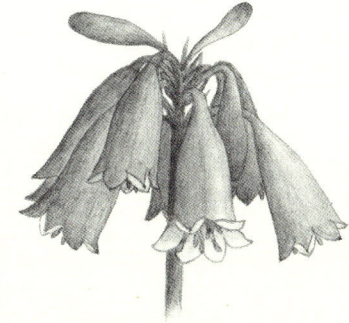

Christmas bells (Blandfordia)

CHAPTER 6
FRANKLIN RIVER SECOND ATTEMPT—1958

Glass canoes

After the first attempt to canoe this formidable river we had no doubt that it would be unwise to tempt fate again. There was little incentive to return to a river which had scared the hell out of us. But then, as the memory of the bad things about it slowly faded, Hawkins and I realised that we couldn't give up.

Above: Framework for the new fibreglass mould.
Opposite: Hawkins and Newland (rear), just above the junction of the Franklin and Collingwood rivers.

Next time we would have to be much better prepared, with attention paid to avoiding past mistakes. Foremost in our preparations would be more suitable craft. We leaned towards a Canadian type canoe because of its buoyancy and capacity to carry bigger loads. (Perhaps it would have been wiser to concentrate on travelling lighter!) The other reason for going Canadian was the introduction of a new material called fibreglass which could be moulded into complex shapes. It was also light, would not corrode, and was just about unbreakable—or so they said. We couldn't wait to try it.

In 1955 Hawkins was a resident doctor at the Launceston General Hospital. In his spare time he experimented with models of canoes, the main criterion being maximum stability. Once satisfied, he built a mould using timber formers and wire netting stretched over these to complete the framework. Professional plasterers then finished off the job of shaping. A coating of fibreglass sealed the plaster, and the mould was ready. He was about to depart to a mainland hospital so I was left with the task of making the first canoe. The only practical way I could do this was to truck the mould to my home at *Blenheim*, Evandale, where I could work on it in my spare time. Aided by several of Hawkins' mates I hauled it up into the loft above the old stables.

It was wintertime and I soon found that on days of high humidity when the resin refused to dry I had to place radiators under the mould to assist the curing. Each coat had to be sanded with a disc grinder to remove irregularities. This was an unpleasant task. The fine grains of glass settled in the pores of the skin, causing severe irritation. I hate to think what it did to my lungs, with only a rudimentary face mask for protection. The design made removal from the mould difficult. The beam at the water-line (four feet) was wider than the deck width (three feet), necessitating cutting the casting almost in halves along the keel line to remove it. After rejoining the halves a tubular steel keel was bonded on over the join.

Next a full deck incorporating two cockpits with spray covers and water-proof hatchlids fore and aft had to be constructed. A full deck on a Canadian canoe was unconventional but we considered this was necessary to cope with the high rainfall and to shed as much water as possible when running rapids. The prototype of the deck would have to be made from aluminium sheet. This was not going to be an easy task as my only tools for the job were an electric drill and tinsnips. Then unexpected help arrived in the form of Henry Crocker, a teacher in sheet metal work at the Hobart Technical College who lived part-time at Evandale. Crocker was able to

Left: During an aerial reconnaissance in 1954, we landed on the beach at Lake Pedder. Hawkins, Dean and pilot Tanner.

RIVERS OF WESTERN TASMANIA

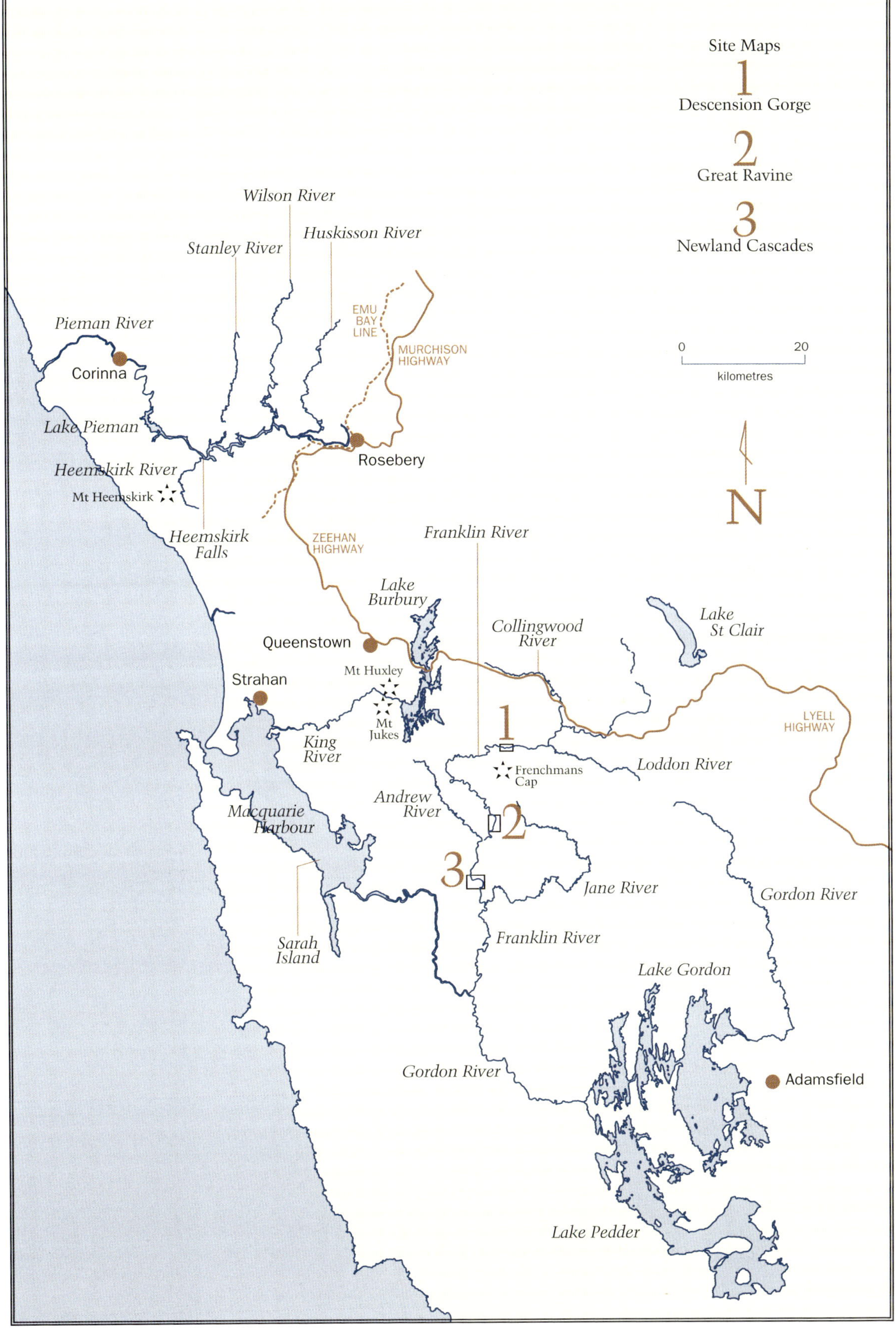

Site Maps

1
Descension Gorge

2
Great Ravine

3
Newland Cascades

0   20
kilometres

N

Pieman River

Corinna

Wilson River

Stanley River

Huskisson River

EMU BAY LINE

MURCHISON HIGHWAY

Lake Pieman

Heemskirk River

Mt Heemskirk

Rosebery

Heemskirk Falls

ZEEHAN HIGHWAY

Franklin River

Lake Burbury

Collingwood River

Lake St Clair

Queenstown

Mt Huxley

LYELL HIGHWAY

Strahan

Mt Jukes

1

Loddon River

King River

Frenchmans Cap

Andrew River

2

Macquarie Harbour

3

Jane River

Gordon River

Franklin River

Sarah Island

Lake Gordon

Adamsfield

Gordon River

Lake Pedder

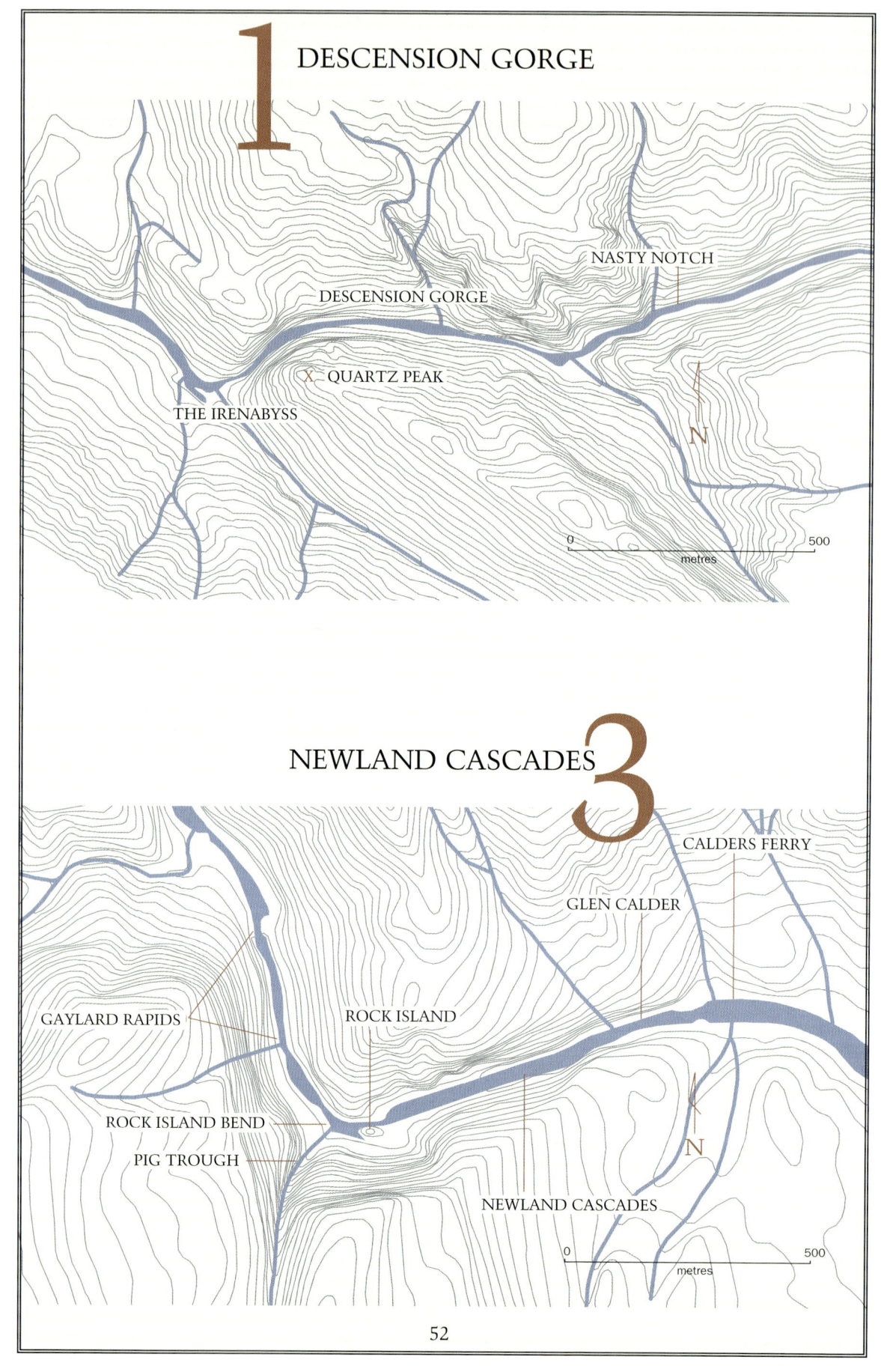

1 DESCENSION GORGE

NASTY NOTCH

DESCENSION GORGE

X QUARTZ PEAK

THE IRENABYSS

N

0 500
metres

NEWLAND CASCADES 3

CALDERS FERRY

GLEN CALDER

GAYLARD RAPIDS

ROCK ISLAND

ROCK ISLAND BEND

PIG TROUGH

N

NEWLAND CASCADES

0 500
metres

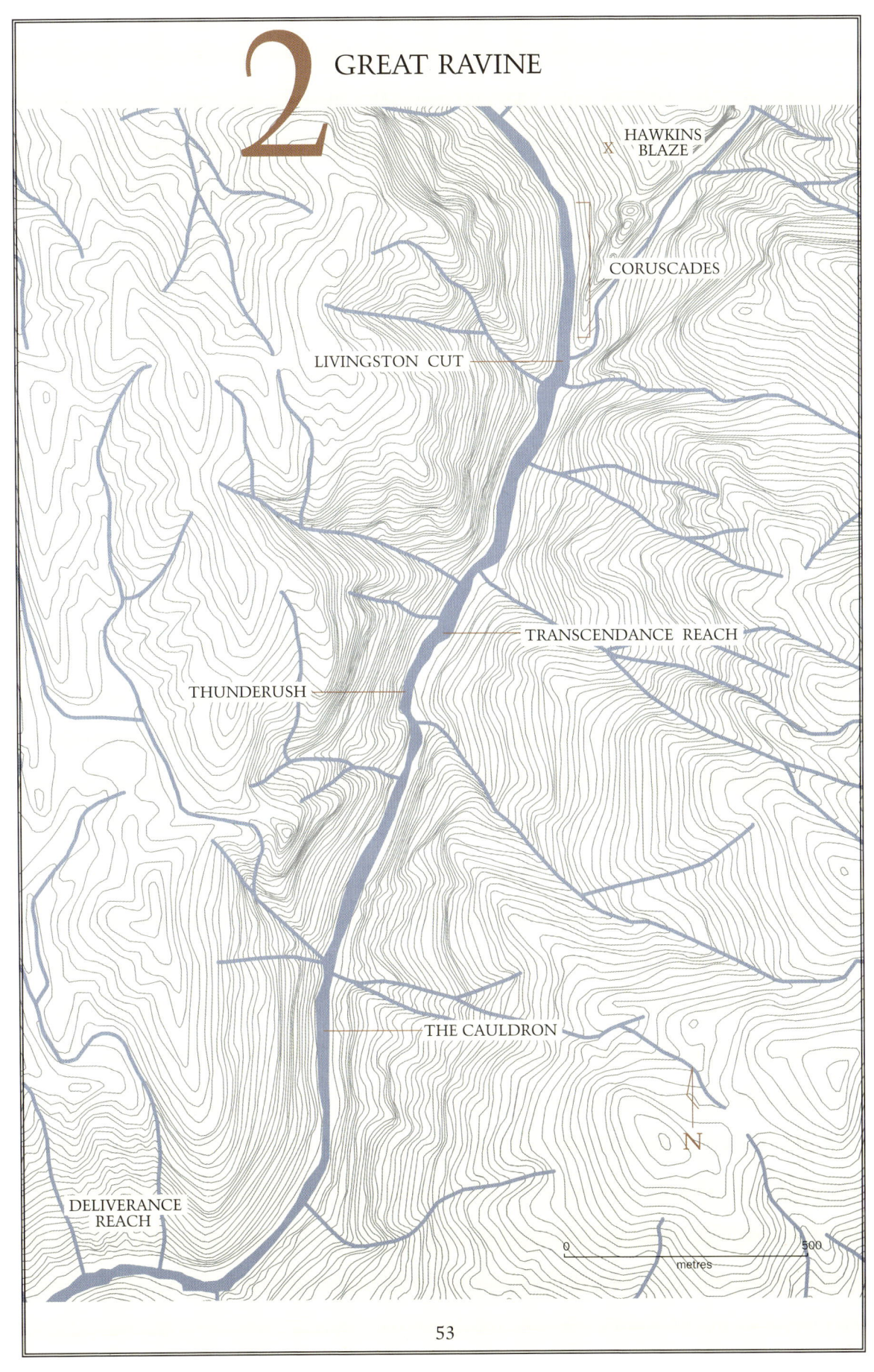

HAWKINS
BLAZE

CORUSCADES

LIVINGSTON CUT

TRANSCENDANCE REACH

THUNDERUSH

THE CAULDRON

N

DELIVERANCE
REACH

0   500

metres

supply two ideal gadgets for the job, a nibbler for cutting around curves and a beading tool for stiffening the sheet metal, so adding a professional touch to the finished product. Later I used this as a mould to make a replacement of fibreglass. In all I used ten gallons (25 litres) of resin to complete the thirteen foot (four metre) long vessel, hence the description '10 gallon canoes' coined by one freelance journalist.

By Christmas 1956 we were ready for a test run. Again the most accessible river was the South Esk. Crocker and I set off from the Rossarden bridge above Fingal. In contrast to our earlier efforts we had a trouble-free run, with no holes and no capsizes. However, we were carrying only a fraction of the load required for the Franklin venture and this proved to be a gap in our testing. What we hadn't foreseen was that the canoe became less stable when carrying big loads. The pronounced 'tumblehome' of the sides made for easier paddling but there was a downside. This was evident when it rolled to one side and it sank deeper, due to decreased area of the canoe above the surface of the water. The destabilising effect was further exacerbated in a cross current, when the flow tended to push down the upstream side.

After the enjoyable break on the South Esk, Crocker agreed to join the 1958 Franklin expedition, and he set about building a canoe the same as mine, except that his was red and mine yellow.

Throughout 1957 Hawkins devoted his spare time to preparing food and equipment. Guided by a dietician, he worked out day-to-day food requirements, each meal for four people going into waterproof plastic bags. Some loaves of bread and wheatmeal biscuits had to be packed into special tins made by Crocker. These were beaded to give extra strength to enable them to withstand an airdrop, and then waterproofed by soldering. Each canoe was equipped with food and gear for four people just in case we lost one again. If this happened in the first few days it might be possible to make use of Weston's folboat, cached in Descension Gorge in 1952.

Neither Weston nor Scarlett was available this time. Hawkins asked Olegas Truchanas of Gordon River fame to accompany us, but with work commitments this was not possible. However he did suggest a fellow bushwalker, Trevor Newland. It was a good choice; he wasn't an experienced canoeist but this was more than made up for by his bushcraft skills, and above all his thorough dependability and good nature. He was always an agreeable companion.

Dean (bow) and Hawkins (stern) in the new fibreglass canoe on the Collingwood River.

Crocker (stern) and Newland (bow) at the junction of the Franklin and Loddon rivers.

December 24, 1957. *The Examiner* newspaper in Launceston reported:

"Adventurous Trip Ahead

Four men in two fibreglass canoes will attempt a 120 mile trip through wild, uninhabited West Coast country next month. Their trip is expected to take 16 days—but they are allowing three weeks for it."

On the day of departure, January 7, 1958, *The Mercury* in Hobart was more dramatic:

"Four Will Challenge Hazardous River

Four adventurous young Tasmanians will set out today to explore Tasmania's 'river of no return'—the hazardous Franklin River."

It had been six years since our first attempt. With years of preparation behind us we were more confident about succeeding this time.

The river level was lower than previously. The heavily laden canoes had to be eased over shallows and portaged around logs and the biggest rapids to lessen the chance of damage. This procedure was not always the best choice, especially when it seemed a good idea to save time and effort by leaving all gear aboard while sliding the canoes over jagged rocks. This often resulted in

minor damage, even if only cracks, and these eventually had to be repaired, so little time was saved.

Entering the gorge where we had taken the cormorant eggs six years earlier, we found fewer birds and nests. Still determined to sample some eggs, we repeated the same antics as last time to get to a nest and take some for the larder. Was it a coincidence that, as before, disaster followed soon afterwards?

This happened just above the infamous stretch of river (Descension Gorge) where Hawkins and I nearly lost our lives in 1952. On this occasion the river was lower and we were confronted by a huge flat rock just above water level, blocking the main channel (Nasty Notch). The solution to our problem seemed simple. Rather than undertake a difficult portage, why not drift the canoe up to the rock, drag it over, and lower it down into the pool below? It was not a hasty decision as we even stopped for lunch before implementing the plan.

We began to lift the bow onto the rock, then before we realised what was happening, the stern was sucked down, the canoe backflipped and slid down into a deep hole, and there it remained, with only a few feet of the bow projecting above the water. Too late we realised that most of the water was finding its way under the rock, and not through the channel on the other side of it. The tremendous suction, combined with pressure from above, firmly wedged the canoe into the narrow shaft. In desperation we all heaved together in an attempt to free it. We may as well have saved our energy. Next we tied one end of a block and tackle rope as high up a tree as we could get and the other end tied to a ring on the bow, and pulled with all our might, at the same time levering with two thirty-foot-long spars, but all to no avail. The canoe was sinking deeper and deeper into the hole. Obviously the forces holding it there were much more than we could cope with.

Somehow we had to alleviate the water pressure bearing down on it. The only way we could do this was to build a dam to divert the water through the other channel. This would be no easy task. The distance between the boulders on either side was 2.5 metres, and the depth two metres, so obviously it was going to take a lot of rock. There was plenty nearby, but not much that was small enough to be of any use. We searched around and found a suitable supply in a gully about 60 metres up. The largest rocks had to be rolled down to where we could manhandle them into place. The smaller ones

Above: Breakfast at Laurel Camp. Four men in a two-man tent. Crocker, Newland and Hawkins.
Opposite: Down the hole at Nasty Notch. Hawkins, Crocker and Newland.

were hurled directly into the gap. Some of these must have lodged inside the canoe, further weakening it. To add to the problem, the canoe was constantly see-sawing back and forth, the pivot point being the base of the huge rock.

It finally broke in halves. The stern section bobbed up in a backwater below. The hatch cover had held and everything was still inside, but a hole in the fibreglass let water in, and the sleeping bags were drenched. A loose day pack containing cooking utensils and Hawkins' medical kit was swept away. This must have been a lapse on his part because previously, whenever you asked for something for a minor complaint, the stock answer was, "I've got just what you need, but it's in the bottom of my pack," indicating that it was stored away so securely that it would be a major undertaking to get to it and if you could do without it he would be grateful.

With half the canoe now gone we thought it would be possible to pull out the bow section (the rope was still tied to it) but no such luck. We continued to build the dam until nightfall. Then rain set in. If the river rose it would be impossible to get close enough to extract the other half. Fortunately it didn't, indicating that the rain was only local. We completed the dam and were then able to pull out the remaining section.

Unless we were prepared to abandon again the idea of canoeing this enigmatic river it was now essential to reach the hut which we knew to be near Mt Fincham. Extra supplies of mending materials were to be airdropped there. We could dry out and live in comfort for a short time while repairing the canoes. The other possibility was that we could retrieve Weston's folboat which had been cached between here and the hut six years earlier. Hopefully Hawkins and I could use this to tow my wreck.

In the meantime, Crocker's canoe would have to carry three people, in addition to most of the gear, while the remains of mine would have to be strung together to make some sort of raft for my use. This was made possible by utilising the two inflatable boat rollers which were carried in the canoe for the dual purpose of providing buoyancy in the event of being swamped, and for portaging. Miraculously, these had not been lost. We left them in their usual position under the gunwales of the stern half, wedged the bow section between them and lashed all together. The stern was now the bow of this unconventional craft! In order to paddle I sat astride up forward. Hawkins was carried amidships on Crocker's canoe. We must have been a strange sight. Of course, this arrangement was only possible where there were no sizeable rapids to negotiate.

That day we reached the spot where we had left Weston's kayak. There was no sign of it, and we surmised that it had been washed away by a massive flood. This was confirmed later by the discovery of the carrybag, caught on an overhanging myrtle branch nearly forty feet above the middle of the river, a few miles downstream. The Franklin had claimed two craft so far, yet we had only covered a quarter of the distance. If we were unsuccessful in rejoining my canoe the score would go to three.

The main picture shows preparations to leave Nasty Notch behind, with the modified vessel on the left. Inset: Retrieving the stern section. Hawkins, Crocker and Newland.

Hawkins recalled:

"We travelled very slowly indeed. We lined Dean's canoe with care for fear it would break apart. In the gorge, lining from those almost sheer cliffs entailed real rockclimbing skill. The first day we made about three-quarters of a mile. The next day, Monday 13th, we dropped about seventy feet in three miles—which gives an idea of the steep descent of the river and the velocity of the current—and passed the (almost) sheer cliff Dean had to climb in 1952 ... Ahead of us now was a difficult stretch of water disappearing round a bend in the gorge and finally—we imagined—ending in the calm pool I had been carried into at the end of my ordeal."

But we still had little idea what lay between the sheer walls of this dark chasm. In 1952 Hawkins had been semi-conscious when swept through here, so only had a vague recollection of what it was like and, faced with the urgency of finding him as quickly as possible, my only thought at the time had been to continue overland down to a bend in the river where I thought there might be a backwater into which he could have been swept. Weston and Scarlett went through here the same year but there did not seem to be any reason to question them about it at the time; we probably had more urgent things on our minds.

To tackle the unknown, with three men in one canoe and me astride my wreck, could be courting disaster and, as lining was well nigh impossible from the cliff tops, Crocker and Newland took the remains of my canoe in tow while Hawkins and I set off to proceed overland. We soon found that the only way to do this was to repeat my previous climb.

Hawkins' impressions of this were much the same as mine.

"What a trip we had. We had to climb a hair-raising cliff about one thousand feet high, much of the face being loose rock. Finally we rejoined our mates. It had taken them about ten minutes to reach the pool. It took Dean and I nearly half a day!"

The tranquil gorge we bypassed is now well known as the Irenabyss (peaceful chasm).

We had hoped to reach the hut before nightfall but with the problem of keeping my wreck in one piece we were forced to stop many times to relash it together. Two or three miles

Rebuilding the canoe at Fincham Crossing.

before our destination the whole contraption collapsed. It was nearly dark and rain had set in once more. We were forced to camp on a rocky ledge. Crocker and Newland managed to get a fire going and sat around it all night. Hawkins was quite comfortable inside a waterproof sleeping bag sheltered by a plastic sheet. I spent the worst night I've ever experienced. I lay inside one half of the wreck and covered myself as best I could with the other half. By morning my sleeping bag was drenched and I was lying in a pool of water. I decided Crocker and Newland made the right choice. A hot mug of tea from their billy revived my spirits. After an hour's paddling the welcome sight of a water level recorder and flying fox over the river confirmed our whereabouts as Fincham Crossing, and we lost no time in making our way up to the hut.

The next three days we worked on the wreck. We trimmed off the longest of the jagged ends of fibreglass and used these pieces to fill the gaps after the two halves were joined. Saplings cut from the bush were shaped to match the curvature of the canoe and bonded inside. A canvas cover took the place of a solid deck, the main function of this being to keep out the water whilst lining over rapids.

The end product was quite a trim craft—two feet shorter than the original —which would have to carry two men and some of their gear. This was a tall order but we had no choice. It was either continue with one and a half canoes, or abandon the attempt. This second option was a serious possibility as we had barely enough food, and most of the resin and fibreglass had been used to rebuild my canoe. However, barring further major disasters, we might just make it.

Then rain plummeted down and the river rose four metres overnight. Intermittent showers continued for the next four days and the river remained a rushing torrent. We were nearly two weeks behind schedule, had covered only a third of the distance and would have to make much faster progress if we were not to starve before we finished. With two men in a one-man canoe, making up for lost time was asking a lot. Lack of freeboard would limit the number of rapids we could run without swamping. We all agreed that we had run out of time.

We hauled the canoes up to a rock ledge and tied them to the recorder framework. Food and gear were left in the hut and we set off to walk out. This time we had a track to follow but it still took two days to reach Queenstown.

The Franklin River would have to wait another year.

Dean paddling half a canoe. Not the ideal way to tackle the Franklin. PHOTO: CROCKER
Following pages: The map used for our 1958 trip, with notes made by Hawkins.

FRENCHMANS CAP

LEGEND

Park Boundary	
Tracks	
Tracks Location Approx. ..	
Roads	
Huts	■
Falls	
Cliffs	
Timber	
Form Lines 250′.	

SCALE: 1 INCH T

This Map is compiled from Air Photos, without
not be regarded as entirely accurate.

Mountain and Track Heights, although not p
information available.

Produced by the Mapping Branch, Lands an

Crown Copyright F

C.M. PITT SURVEYOR

Handwritten annotations:

FOUND
CARRYING BAG OF
CANOE LEFT IN
1951 30′ UP IN
TREE.

BECAUSE OF BAD
WEATHER
SPENT
FROM
Jan 15th
to 21st
HERE
Mending
CANOE.

OF WELTONS

END OF GORGE WHERE WASHED UP
LUNCHED HERE 1958 at LA

SITE OF
OLD HUT
WHERE
CANOE
LEFT
IN 1951
WALK
OUT

SITE OF
1951 BLUNDER
-LOST CANOE.
1000′ climb

CAMP

14 MILES TO
DIVIDE
HUT
20/1/58

HEC
HUT
CAMPS
X, XI, XII
XIII, XIV
XV.

LUNCH

CEDAR
HUT

GORGE

CAMP VII

GOOD
GOING

GORGE

CAMP
IX
(Ph)
(-Rain)

JAMMED
CANOE
CANOE
WRECK
LOST

WATER
GAUGE
PLAYING
FOX

MT. FINCHAM
△ 2680′

Wyld River

Canyon River

Wright River

FRANKLIN RIVER

FRANKLIN

BURNT ENGINEER RANGE

ANDREW

BURNT TIMBER RANGE

River

Looker

RIVER

BURNT TIMBER

BURNT TIMBER RANGE

RIVER

Lake Nancy

Lake
Gwendolen

Lions Head
Nth Cook

Jetty L

FRENCHMANS
CAP 4756

E. Tahu

CLYTEMNAESTRA

Lake
Mill

Livingston

DECEPTION P

Abt.
10° 25′

TRUE NORTH   MAG. NORTH

800

42°15′

790

42°20′

370

1485

380

50′

295

285

070

145 45′

380

50′

Livingston Rivulet

Serenity Research

Hawkins Blaze

Thunderush

The Cauldron

"This hideous defile"

With so much time, energy and money spent on overcoming the whims of this intractable river, we were now too committed to give up. Besides, for once luck must be with us.

Above: Crocker, Newland, Dean, Hawkins. THE MERCURY 24 JANUARY 1958
Left: The Great Ravine.

The plan was for Crocker and Newland to walk into Fincham Hut, while Hawkins and I would once more set forth down the Collingwood, this time in Hawkins' canoe which he had cast from the same mould. By now we realised that travelling lighter was the answer to a lot of our problems. On board were enough supplies to last just one week, the maximum time allowed to reach Fincham Hut, where we would be re-supplied by means of an airdrop.

One piece of equipment added to our load was a transceiver with morse key, headphones and aerial, all of which Hawkins picked up at army disposals, his main source of equipment and clothing. He hoped to be in regular contact with Hobart Radio to report our progress. It could also be useful in emergencies. When communicating Hawkins referred to a coded map, which was duplicated for the recipient. Friends, advised when we were due to arrive at the hut, would come in to meet us and take out with them our exposed films and any messages. Elaborate preparations, however, were no guarantee of success.

On December 15, 1958 Hawkins and I set off under overcast skies in swirling dark water which did nothing to increase our confidence in being able to succeed this time. At our first camp we erected the aerial and commenced tapping out a message in Morse code. No reply. Were we getting through? Next camp, still no response, confirming that the radio was not working. In spite of careful planning we would have no communication with the outside world.

After four days of battling in persistent rain on a rising river we camped early under a cliff overhang which sheltered the tent from most of the rain. Hawkins slept in an army hammock, complete with waterproof roof. I could never make myself comfortable in these things, preferring to lie flat on solid ground. I also had the satisfaction of being able to poke him with a paddle and threaten to tip him out if he slept in.

Next day the river looked even more sinister. It had risen another two metres overnight. The hazardous long gorge that nearly cost our lives seven years earlier lay ahead. Even though we were already behind schedule, we decided to stay put. This was when the radio would have been useful to contact the other two and advise them of a possible late arrival. The one thing that lifted our spirits was keeping the fire going and boiling the billy under the shelter of the rock face.

At daylight we anxiously scanned the river. There was little change; it was just as high. We could not delay further. As soon as the rain eased we righted the canoe where it had been tipped upside down to keep out the downpour, and loaded up. It would have been safer to haul it up to the campsite but there had been no room on the rocky ledge. We had been weatherbound for a day and a half and would now have to make up for lost time.

Looking back I am forced to conclude that we were either accident prone, incompetent, or both. We had not advanced very far before we were in serious trouble again.

The swift current threatened to sweep us onto a huge log jutting out from the bank into midstream. We could possibly have paddled around the end of this, but once out in the main flow would have found it difficult to stop before rapids in the gorge took hold, so we hurriedly made for the bank and attempted to line the canoe around it. However, we underestimated the strength of the current and the canoe was swept sideways onto the obstruction. Held by this, it tipped over and rapidly filled. We crawled out along the log and tried to pull it ashore. We should have realised this was futile. We couldn't budge it. Meanwhile, the side of the canoe against the snag was caving in under the tremendous water pressure.

We carried with us a small block and tackle for such emergencies. This had been carefully stowed away inside the aft hatch, the one now furthest away from the bank. Normally it would have been a simple matter to get it out. However, the canoe was upside down, and almost totally submerged. In order to reach the hatch and undo the spring-loaded cover I had to swim underneath the canoe and wrestle with the fastening to get the cover off, and after several submersions, finally succeeded. Between us we managed to locate what we were looking for, all the while taking precautions to prevent other gear from falling out. We tied one rope to a tree, and the other to the bow, and lifted the canoe sufficiently for us to manhandle it over the log. What we pulled ashore could be described as nothing but a wreck. The only things keeping it afloat were the watertight compartments fore and aft and the inflated boat rollers amidships. The fibreglass was fractured over a large area and also had a hole big enough to crawl through.

Our situation was desperate, night was falling and typical west coast drizzle had set in. We stood a good chance of being washed away before morning, especially as our campsite was on a small sandy beach, only inches above river level, and a steep bank covered with dense jungle prevented us from getting to higher ground. All we could do was hope that the rain was local. If it rained upstream we would be in serious trouble.

We covered the canoe as best we could with a plastic sheet and, aided by

Hawkins checking our all-night repairs, and inspecting the scene of the disaster next morning.

heat from a fire which we somehow managed to get going, dried the area to be repaired. Working by fire and candlelight we set about cutting marine plywood to fill the hole. This was bonded into place with fibreglass cloth and matte impregnated with epoxy resin. By daylight the job was completed. A quick snack and we were off again.

The river hadn't risen, nor had it fallen. It was fast and dangerous and we still had to get through the gorge that had previously caused us so much trouble. Conditions were ominously similar to those during the first attempt. We would play safe, lining and portaging to avoid the worst rapids. However, this was not without its own hazards, especially when we were forced to balance on rocky ledges, or jump from one slippery boulder to another. After a strenuous day, during which we seemed to be as much in the water as out, we camped under some Huon pines. Some of these had burls on their trunks, and reminded me of a Canadian pine forest with black bears clinging to them. After a hearty meal we collapsed into our sleeping bags.

Still trying to get back on schedule, we rose at 4.30 am and peered through the fog to ascertain the state of the river. It had fallen a few centimetres but still looked threatening. Today would be the big test. Would we manage to make it through the gorge this time?

We reached the cliffs where we had taken cormorant eggs on two previous occasions. This time there were no birds to be seen. Had a late flood taken their nests or had we scared them off when we took some eggs? Then we were in Descension Gorge which, after two disasters, we had come to dread.

We started lining over the biggest of the rapids. Hawkins slipped in. Fortunately I was downstream and was able to grab him before he was swept away. Was this a bad omen? Was the curse of the cormorants still with us?

Soon afterwards we encountered a sheer cliff rising hundreds of feet on our side of the river. With no possibility of being able to line from here, the only alternative was to cross over. To make a controlled crossing in fast water it is necessary to head the canoe upstream and paddle furiously to hold your own against the current, at the same time slightly angling the bow to the flow so that the canoe is gradually carried to the other side. We judged it well and finished up against rocks where we intended to land. But then we found we couldn't keep hold of the slippery rocks, and before we could do anything to prevent it happening, the bow swung out into midstream and we were in danger of being swept broadside against rocks at the entrance to the gorge. Fortunately we both reacted the same way and straightened in time to avoid this.

While the immediate danger was past, we were now committed to going down the gorge—*backwards*. Normally we still would have had some control by looking behind over our shoulders, but today was no different to the others in that we wore parkas to keep out the incessant drizzle, and the hoods over our heads tied tightly under our chins proved to be effective blinkers preventing us turning around far enough to see behind. There was no time to undo them. We were too preoccupied.

FOOD LIST - 3 Man Walking Party from Queenstown Road
to Fincham Hut.
3 day allowance till air drop
GROUP "B"

Bread - presliced (1 loaf per day)	3
Butter	1 lb.
Eggs (1 per day + 1 doz. for use at hut)	21
Bacon (rasher per day)	9 rashers
Salt	¼ lb.
Cheese 2 oz. per person per day	9 pieces
Honey M & B tin	1 lb.
Biscuits - wheat flake	1 pkt
Meat (steak	1½ lbs
(Sausages	1 doz
Raisins	12 oz. pkt
Dates	1 lb.
Dried vegs (Peas) use Hut's	
Hut well (Carrots)	
supplied (Onions (1 meal	1 pkt
(Potatoes (at	1 pkt
(Divide Hut	
Dried fruit (½ lb. = meal for 3) 3 x ½	1½ lbs.
Dried soups (mixed)	3 pkts
Powdered milk	1 tin
Sugar (1/3 lb per person per day	3 lbs.
Oxo cubes	1 tin
Tea	¼ lb.
Chocolate ¼ lb. per day	¾ lb.
Barley sugar	1 pkt
Nuts 1 pkt per day	3 pkts
Dripping	¼ lb.
Vegemite (small)	1
Matches	3 boxes

2 oz. BONOX.

5 ITEMS

Food supplies, organised by Hawkins with Crocker's assistance.

69

FOOD LIST - 3 People for 4 days.
Air drop to Fincham Hut

GROUP "C"

Item	Amount
Bread (presliced - 1 loaf per day	4
Butter (12 oz. tins)	2
Eggs (carried in by walking party	12
Salt	1 lb.
Cheese 2 oz. wedges (1 per person per day)	12
Honey 1 M & B tin	1 lb.
Biscuits (1 pkt per day wheatflake)	4
Sardines (large)	2 tins
Tinned meat (mixed)	6
Tinned peas (large	2
Tinned beans (large)	3
Peanut butter (jars - large)	1
Oat	1 lb.
Dates	1
Raisins	1
Dried vege. - Peas) use huts	
Carrots)	
Beer tins	4
Meth. spirits plastic bottle	20 ozs.
Tinned cream small	2
Dried onions	2 pkts
Dried fruit - (apples	1 lb.
(½ lb. per meal (nectarines	
for 4 (peaches	2
Dried soups (mixed) pkts	
(1 pkt per meal)	4
Powdered milk tin	1
Sugar	4 lbs.
Flour	2 lbs.
Tomato sauce (small bottle - M & B tin) (Plastic Cont)	
Matches (1 per person	12
Tinned fruit - small	1 lb.
Meat & vegs. tin	4
Tea	1
Nescafe	1½ lb.
Chocolate ½ lb. per day	1
Sweets (mixed)	1 lb.
Rolled oats	1 lb.
Nuts (1 pkt per day)	1 lb.
Dripping	4
Matches	½ lb.
	6 boxes

It wasn't quite like this!
Southern Tasmanian Aero
Club cartoon, 1959.

Hawkins later wrote:

"In the next few minutes we lived a lifetime … We began a terrifying race backwards down the rushing rapids of the gorge. This is it. We've had it, I recall saying to myself. We were powerless. All we could do was to keep the bow pointing upstream as we raced madly down river, lurching over waterfalls in sickening swoops, burrowing stern first at the foot of each fall … I was in the stern and remember seeing Dean rise several feet above me as we lunged over each fall, the canoe standing almost vertically, as I was engulfed in icy waves. With every successive blow to my back my breath was torn from me, and every time we plunged down a fall I thought it would be our last. We must have been travelling at about 20 m.p.h. (32 kph) and always backwards. It was a miracle that we weren't smashed at the foot of one of the falls."

There was absolutely nothing we could do except fight to keep the craft facing upstream and hope it would find its own way through the clearest passage and not be brought to a stop by either wedging itself at the base of a fall or smashing into a rock. Paradoxically, travelling backwards might have been the reason we were spared the former fate.

The canoe had been designed with a blunter stern than bow for streamlining purposes and under the present conditions this configuration was an advantage because it provided more buoyancy where it mattered. Nevertheless it seemed to take ages before we emerged from the trough under each fall, and even with the storm covers tied around our waists, water rushed in. Why we didn't capsize I'll never know.

Balancing a canoe full of water is about as difficult as riding a log. By now the deck was only just above water level. Each time it lurched to one side I thought it would be the last, and it seemed to be ages before it righted itself, but amazingly we did make it into calmer water just above the Irenabyss. We cautiously turned and paddled towards some rocks and carefully stepped ashore. Here we engaged in some back slapping, congratulating each other on having survived.

This time the Irenabyss held no terrors for us. We now knew that its dark waters ran deep and silent through a sheer sided chasm, so after baling out the canoe we paddled through to the backwater where Hawkins had been washed ashore in 1952. Here we lit a fire, thawed out, and enjoyed a hot meal. Again, it was good to be alive!

We pushed on further down the fast river. By late afternoon I was beginning to wonder if we would achieve our goal before nightfall. In the eerie half light water cascading down the sides of the gorges reminded me ominously of the enforced bivouac the previous summer when we just failed to reach Fincham Hut before nightfall. I had no intention of repeating that miserable experience. I paddled all the harder. Fortune favoured us. Rounding the last bend we spied Newland waiting for us at the bottom of the track leading up to the hut. We had arrived on the deadline, one week after setting out. Crocker prepared a welcome hot meal.

While Hawkins and I were coming downriver, Crocker and Newland hadn't been idle. They completed repairs to the canoes, listed supplies and apportioned the loads. Next day Hawkins and Crocker found the fault in the transceiver, and re-soldered a broken connection. We contacted the Southern Tasmanian Aero Club and arranged an airdrop of mending materials and the balance of the food supplies. These were dropped the same day.

So we set off in three canoes; Crocker and Newland in theirs, Hawkins in his, and I in my shortened version. An extra canoe made progress all the slower when portaging, as more often than not all four would have to manhandle each canoe in turn. After two weeks of backbreaking work, relieved somewhat by some exciting canoeing, we were well on our way down this wild river when I nearly met my Waterloo.

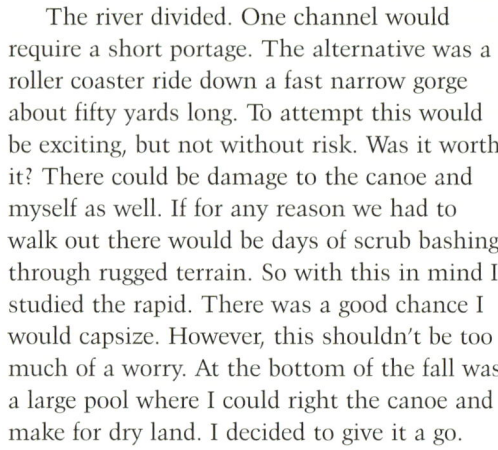

The river divided. One channel would require a short portage. The alternative was a roller coaster ride down a fast narrow gorge about fifty yards long. To attempt this would be exciting, but not without risk. Was it worth it? There could be damage to the canoe and myself as well. If for any reason we had to walk out there would be days of scrub bashing through rugged terrain. So with this in mind I studied the rapid. There was a good chance I would capsize. However, this shouldn't be too much of a worry. At the bottom of the fall was a large pool where I could right the canoe and make for dry land. I decided to give it a go.

The dark tea-coloured water whitened where it entered the ravine. Thrust forward at ever increasing speed and buffeted by cross currents, the shortened canoe swung from side to side, and not having yet mastered the new handling characteristics, I found it difficult to control. I was heading towards a large rock which extended into midstream from the left bank. In order to get around it I was forced to head for the opposite side with the intention of straightening up only at the last moment to

Top: The master craftsman: Crocker burning holes in boxes for rope handles at Fincham Hut. PHOTO: NEWLAND
Bottom: The smoke bomb let off to guide the pilot for our airdrop. Newland is on the lookout, on top of the hut chimney. PHOTO: CROCKER
Opposite: Portaging exit to The Cauldron.

get back on course. But I didn't see a low rock at the base of the cliff on the right side until it was too late. The bow jammed between this and the cliff face, the stern whipped around and smashed into the rock I had been trying to avoid in the first place, and I was now held broadside on to the raging torrent. The canoe filled rapidly, half capsized, and remained jammed in this position. I tried desperately to escape but found myself powerless against the torrent. Fortunately, the buoyancy provided by my life jacket assisted in keeping my head above water for most of the time. However, no matter how much I struggled, I could not get out. I cannot say how long I persevered, but I knew that I was getting weaker every minute and that if I didn't succeed somehow soon I would surely drown.

It probably seems obvious that all I had to do was to stop fighting the current, drop down and go with it. But it was not as simple as that. If, when I let go, I were to be trapped between the large rock and the canoe, my last chance of escape would be gone. The result would be the same if there was not enough space between the canoe and the river bottom. Still, there was nothing else for it. With a mighty heave I pushed myself down below the canoe. What a relief! The way was clear. But then it seemed I would never

Serenity Reach, showing Hawkins Blaze in the middle distance.

emerge again. The aerated water didn't provide much buoyancy. Not until I reached the end of the rapid and surfaced was I able to refill my aching lungs. Maybe it was fortunate that I used to practice swimming underwater across the local river at Evandale.

My first reaction was relief at having survived. Next came anger. This had been one more life-threatening situation which could have been avoided if I had not been so foolhardy. But then, if you didn't take some risks, a trip degenerated into boredom. It seemed that whatever I did I couldn't win. The strain of 'beating' this river was getting to me.

The next problem was to free the canoe. It remained jammed by the fierce current and would require mechanical assistance to extricate it, so one end of the block and tackle was attached to a large boulder on top of the cliff and the other end to a ring on the bow. When we began to pull, the rope had to be held away from the rock face to prevent it fraying, as it was under considerable tension. As soon as the bow was lifted high enough for it to clear the rock wedging it, the canoe began its headlong dash down the ravine and the rope holding it was let run free so that the craft could find its way to the pool below where Hawkins was waiting. I suppose it says something for our workmanship that when we inspected the canoe there was no major damage and all gear was still intact inside the two hatches.

Soon we encountered a small log jam barring our way. Vicious looking sharp stakes protruded from the tangled mass. Rather than damage our canoes and use precious mending materials we decided on a novel approach. This obstruction seemed as good an excuse as any to try something new, and at the same time avoid portaging. Newland was an expert in the use of gelignite for blasting, and had brought some along with him. He tied a few sticks of this to the end of a long spar, connected a fuse wire and pushed them under water. We stood back while he lit the fuse. When the gelignite exploded spray filled the air and bits of debris fell back into the water. The way was clear. We could have portaged, but this was much more fun. We continued on our way.

Below: Gelignite Trevor places charges. Ignition! Passage cleared.

The river followed a sinuous course with rapids no more than a kilometre apart and it was often necessary to portage around these to avoid possible damage. We were running short of mending materials and had to conserve what was left until the next airdrop. Consequently, incredible as it may sound, it took us three weeks to reach The Churn, the biggest single drop on the river, and the beginning of the Great Ravine. Here we spent most of the day cutting a track through scrub across the inside of the bend and carrying gear down to where we could launch the canoes into Serenity Reach, a magnificent sanctuary of calm water bounded on each side by high hills. At the far end of the sound is the Livingston Cut where the Livingston Rivulet joins the Franklin from the east and, just before that, the great white rock slope on the eastern wall of the ravine now named Hawkins Blaze.

We camped not far below The Churn, and next morning Hawkins and I walked back up to photograph it. We spotted a large black cormorant on a rock, waiting its chance to swoop down after fish disorientated by the turbulent water. Quite irrationally, we now associated cormorants with bad luck and we had no hesitation in shooting this one. It fell into the water and floated down towards us. When we pulled it out to examine it we were surprised at its size. Our bad luck associated with cormorants returned.

Crocker and Newland take off.

We waited for most of the day for a prearranged airdrop of mending materials. The pilot could not believe that we were still so far upriver and thought he had missed us. He returned to Hobart with our vital supplies. We were now desperately short of fibreglass and resin to repair battered canoes. This meant travelling all the more carefully to avoid further damage.

For the next four days we portaged around the worst of the rapids and were almost through the Great Ravine when we were confronted with a situation which we had feared all along—to be trapped in a gorge with no escape, except by going forwards through a set of horror rapids.

Ahead lay a deep chasm with vertical walls. Not far ahead around a bend we could hear the thunder of rapids. We had to investigate what lay there before proceeding, and it seemed the only way was to climb above the cliffs to get a view. However, this was impractical on the right side because the cliffs rose hundreds of feet into the sky, and the precipitous left side was covered with thick scrub down to flood level, about forty feet up. Cutting a track through here would take many hours and be quite dangerous. We had to find another way.

I tied one end of a hundred-foot long rope to a log in the river and the other end to the canoe and cautiously eased my way around a blind corner. Even with the current getting stronger, everything was under control until I noticed that the rope was caught under a wood screw which had inadvertently been left sticking out during the re-joining of the canoe halves. I couldn't flick it off because there was too much tension to allow this. The pressure on the screw was considerable and I hoped, with a bit of luck, that it would give way. But no, it held firm. The result was that the canoe tipped sufficiently for water to rush in. With the extra weight straining it, the rope began to fray where it was caught. I was heading for a 'widow maker' set of rapids; if the rope parted I would be swept down into a nasty looking hole, where I could easily be trapped. I was on the brink of the fearsome fall now known as The Cauldron. I leapt out onto a submerged rock beneath the cliff on the left side of the river. The canoe remained held just under the surface and almost close enough for me to grab it. I had to make a decision. Was it worth risking my life? Should I make a desperate effort to get a hold of the rope and pull it out? I might succeed. But then there was a good chance that I might not, lose my balance, slip, and be swept over the brink. I decided that 'discretion is the better part of valour'.

The rope broke. The canoe raced away down the rapid, crashed into a huge boulder and broke into halves—again! The stern section remained jammed under a five foot fall while the bow half containing my clothes and sleeping bag continued on, and tumbled over an even bigger drop. It, too, was held fast against a boulder.

Now that I was around the corner I could see that it would be possible to land on low flat rocks on the other side. I let the others know and they drifted their canoes down and pulled them up onto these. There was nowhere for them to land on my side so I was stranded.

Hawkins recounted:

"In driving squalls we began to toss gelignite charges with short fuses upstream in the hope a blast would blow the stern free to some place further on, where we would have access to the gear inside. In the meantime, Dean standing on a rock at the foot of the rapid, past the waterfall in which it was jammed, was ready to dive into the river and grab the stern should this be blown clear. It was very cold and it must have been freezing for Dean on his rocky perch. Fortunately, the distance between us was only about forty feet (12 metres) and so we were able to toss him an occasional can of hot coffee and food heated on a primus. For six hours we toiled in the driving rain and cold, and when darkness fell the bow and stern were still jammed and we were almost frozen.

A thunderstorm was upon us, the thunder booming in the gorge and the rain beating down as we threw a rope to Dean and pulled him back to our side of the river." [10]

We cleared a rough campsite and prepared for another miserable night. Like Calder, I wished I had never encountered 'this hideous defile'.

However, next day we woke to a fine misty sunrise. Overnight the canoe's stern section had floated out into a backwater not far below. I retrieved wet clothes and a sleeping bag. Once more camera and films were ruined. The rest of the day was taken up lowering the other two canoes down the remaining falls.

These were the last major obstacles in this treacherous gorge we called Deception Gorge because of its proximity to the Deception Range to the east and also because the name seemed to fit. The Deception Range was so named by Calder in 1840 "from the frequency with which I was foiled, or deceived in my attempts to lead the path across them". [11] We too felt we had

Previous pages: Dean with his back to the wall at The Cauldron. A rope is tied to the canoe, submerged in front of him. While stranded here for many hours, Dean was thrown the occasional can of hot coffee and heated food.
Top left: Newland in the froth at the Great Ravine.
Left: The view north to Clytemnestra and Frenchmans Cap.
PHOTO: CROCKER

been 'deceived' in our efforts to get through the gorge. The official name, also from Calder's description, is now the Great Ravine. It is ten kilometres long and we laboured all of six days to portage its many falls, descending a hundred metres in the process.

When in 1939 Reg Morrison and his companions entered this gorge for the first time by boat they were looking for Huon pine that they could fell and float downstream. It took them ten days to drag their punt, laden with supplies, *upriver* through the rapids! A remarkable achievement. They chose to do it the hard way because they were told by another piner, who claimed to know the area, that if they attempted to go downstream they stood a good chance of being swept over a one hundred foot waterfall. In light of the piners' feat, the time that we took to get through seems excessive.

One reason for our slow progress can be put down to fatigue. We were fit young men but weeks of never ending toil and mental strain brought about by the uncertainty of what dangers lay ahead was taking its toll. At times we were not as patient with each other as we could have been, and were becoming rather despondent. "One of us could easily die before we get through," remarked Hawkins, to which another member of the party responded that he had no intention of obliging!

Having read this far it must seem that we were preoccupied with coping with one disaster after another, but this is not the whole story. I am pleased

Transcendence Reach, looking back to Livingston Cut and the top section of Hawkins Blaze.

to say that we were able to rise above the trauma of these events and from time to time enjoy the surroundings. Some parts of the river were a delight, especially on days when the sun shone and we didn't mind getting wet. In the midst of incredible beauty it was not hard to believe we were in another world. Such a place is Transcendence Reach, below The Coruscades in the Great Ravine, truly 'beyond the sphere of experience'. Apart from the murmur of rapids in the distance, the only other sound was the call of the crescent honeyeater, its loud and melodic "Egypt" song carrying over the peaceful water. The view looking back upriver from the southern end of this reach is awe inspiring. There is so much of interest that even the most amateurish of artists or photographers could produce a masterpiece. In the foreground white quartz escarpments on both banks rise up from the dark, slow flowing river. Upstream, white-blossomed leatherwoods grow in profusion on the steep slopes on the left, while gregarious pointed pines thrive close to the river on the gently rising slope of the opposite bank. In the distance the Livingston Rivulet silently enters the Franklin through a narrow chasm under an overhanging cliff. Ridges along the tops of the cliffs appear to be snow-covered with their white quartz capping.

The most prominent landmark is Hawkins Blaze, an inverted V of white quartz. From Transcendence Reach you can only see the apex above the intervening hills forming the southern bank of the river where it changes direction from east to south. Some time in the past fire had destroyed the vegetation holding the thin layer of soil on the steep slope, which was then eroded by the heavy rains, leaving a bare rock face. Huge slabs of quartz have

Portaging in the Great Ravine.

broken away from the bottom, creating one of the longest rapids on the river, now known as the The Coruscades or 'sparkling waterfalls'.

Once out of the confines of the Great Ravine we were in a different world. The Andrew River entering at Rafters Basin swelled the flow of a wider and more sedate river which gradually slackened its pace, making it possible to relax and gaze around as we drifted along under the shade of the rain forest. The dominant myrtle was a constant source of delight, the foliage ranging from 'richest russet to emerald green'. The wildlife seemed to enjoy sharing with us the pleasant surroundings. Cockatoos, both black and white, appeared overhead, and honeyeaters busied themselves flitting between the distinctive smelling flowers of the leatherwood trees.

We travelled more lightly now, and were able to paddle for long distances without having to portage. Twenty kilometres was the most covered in one day, the distance from the Newland Cascades to the Jane River Hut. This is several kilometres below the Jane River junction, and is usually accessed by a track from Eagle Creek, a tributary of the lower Gordon. The hut was built by the Hydro-Electric Commission for use by hydrographers intending their data to be used to support damming the Franklin River. Oh, what luxury to sleep on bunks in their hut, and yarn around a fire in comfort. We quickly adjusted to this lifestyle and decided to have a rest day here. This meant an even longer paddle to meet the tourist launch at Marble Cliffs on the Gordon River next day, but we thought it would be worth it.

Before dawn we stumbled down the steep, slippery bank, studded with low stumps, the right height to trip the unwary and send them flying. We loaded the last of the gear, hopped in and went through the first rapid in semi-darkness. We were now on part of the river with features named by the piners when they came upriver from the Gordon.

The first major obstacle they encountered was Big Fall, and the second Double Fall. Both are easily portaged going downstream. We were tempted to shoot Big Fall but there was something about it that made us uneasy, even though it didn't appear to be as difficult as some others we had shot without getting into serious trouble. The first canoe lined over came to a sudden stop when it struck a ledge below water, swung around and capsized. It remained broadside on under the fall, which proved to be a real 'stopper'. Fortunately, we were able to haul the canoe away with little damage done. If we had attempted to shoot this rapid it might have been a different story. For once we had done something right! (Unfortunately, two people have since drowned here.)

A few kilometres on we sighted Pyramid Island at the junction of the Gordon and Franklin. The small landmark was given this name in the days of the convict piners because the foliage resembled a pyramid, but now floods have largely denuded it. When Hawkins and I viewed this island from the air, prior to our first attempt to canoe the Franklin, I thought that if we ever reached here, there should be a celebration. Well, we had arrived, and I insisted on a stop to boil the billy.

The first recorded sighting of the Franklin River was by Thomas Scott here in 1824. He did not name the river but showed it on his map. Between one and four years later James Butler, the Commandant of Sarah Island penal settlement, explored the area. When he came to the confluence of the two rivers he was not sure which was the Gordon and which the Franklin, so the Franklin again remained unnamed. It was left to Calder to name it in 1840, when he encountered it in the Great Ravine.[12]

We hurried on down the Gordon and waited a short time beneath the towering Marble Cliffs before the *J. Lee M.* arrived. Curious tourists gazed down on four bearded, suntanned, wild-looking men in their battered red and yellow canoes. Reg Morrison welcomed us aboard and took our canoes in tow. We appreciated the free lunch served while cruising the remaining section of the river and then crossing Macquarie Harbour. Arriving at Strahan, we made for the Bay View Hotel in time for dinner! The proprietor, Mr Stubbs, announced to the assembled guests that we were the first men to canoe the Franklin River, and invited us to dine 'on the house'. When the menu came around Hawkins just said, "Yes, please." We all followed suit, and celebrated with the biggest meal for weeks!

Sadly, this was the last time that we were all together. Trevor Newland died in an industrial accident in 1974. The Newland Cascades which tumble down a wide, beautiful gorge of the Franklin, with fascinating rock formations on each side, are a fitting memorial to him.

Henry Crocker felt that he 'had done enough canoeing to last a lifetime' and did not return to the Franklin. Hawkins and I revisited the lower half several times, he in order to complete a film about river canoeing, and I to show my family the wonders of a river which was about to disappear forever—or so we thought.

Canoeists arrive after hazardous river trip

Left: Wreckage below The Cauldron. Half a canoe in the foreground. PHOTO: CROCKER
Opposite: Hawkins negotiating the ravine where Dean met his Waterloo.

Rendezvous with the J. Lee M. at the Marble Cliffs, Gordon River.

Newland and Crocker at Fincham Hut.

Below: Lining the Big Fall. PHOTO: CROCKER

The heroes: Crocker, Newland, Dean, Hawkins.

Hawkins and canoe at Nasty Notch.

Dean and Newland relax at Fincham Hut.

*Wireless operators,
New Year's Day.*
PHOTO: CROCKER

*Outside the Bay View
Hotel, Strahan.*

WHITE
WATER
HEROES

*Dean's canoe
still trapped after
his escape.*

*New Year's Day camp 1959:
Hawkins, with hammock,
and Crocker.*

*Dean and Newland retrieving
gear below The Cauldron.*

TASMANIA'S DAILY NEWSPAPER

JANUARY 15, 1959

CANOEISTS FINISH MOST HAZARDOUS RIVER "EXCURSION"

Four canoeists arrived in Macquarie Harbor yesterday, tired, but safe, after completing one of the most hazardous river journeys ever attempted in Tasmania.

120-MILE JOURNEY UNIQUE

Their dangerous journey started about three weeks ago 1100 feet above sea level and took them along the Franklin and Gordon Rivers. It was the first time the 120-mile journey had ever been covered by canoe.

The four adventurers, whose previous attempts had failed, are Dr. John Hawkins (21), pilot, of the Royal Hobart Hospital, Mr. John Dean (22), mechanic, of Evandale, Mr. Trevor Newland (about 30), boilermaker, and Mr. Henry Crocker (about 34), wharf teacher, both of Hobart.

ONE RESC... THREE DR...

SYDNEY. — A seaman who... was rescued by a fishing traw... from a freighter off Ulla... New South Wales yester...

FOUR CANOEISTS MAK... SLOW PROGRESS

...thought Victim Murder

London's Worst Fog For Weeks

LONDON. — Ice and fog caused traffic hold-ups throughout Britain yesterday morning, and London had its worst fog for many weeks.

C.M.L. CHIEFS HERE

SENIOR executives of the City Mutual Life Assurance Society Ltd. were yesterday entertained at a dinner at Wrest Point Hotel by the Hobart branch of the society.

Britain Wants Sub Returned

JOURNEY ...ER FOR ...ANOEISTS

...ists arrived in Macquarie Harbour yester... ...t safe after completing one of the most ...river journeys ever attempted in Tasmania.

...AND DRAW

Doing the Splits
the easy way

After finally 'conquering' the Franklin, Hawkins and I turned our attention to the Gordon. We were interested in exploring the upper section from the Gordon Bend to the Serpentine junction. The remainder had been canoed by Olegas Truchanas on his second attempt in 1958.

Above: Typical reach of the middle Gordon.
Opposite: Looking upstream towards the site of the present Gordon Dam.

The Mercury, January 14, 1961:

"Canoeists Will Face Hazards to Explore River in West

Two men, Dr. John Hawkins of Hobart and Mr. John Dean of Evandale, will attempt a 100 mile trip in two canoes down the Gordon River.

Today they will leave Hobart with about 20 young people (members of the Hobart Walking Club) who will assist with the canoes and gear as far as the Gordon River about five miles beyond Adamsfield.

At Maydena they will travel by Landrovers and a VW 24 miles to Adamsfield. From here the party will assist with carrying a kayak and a fibreglass canoe over the final five miles to the banks of the Gordon.

If the men accomplish the feat it will be the first time that canoeists have made the trip from the upper reaches of the river.

The men aim to reach Strahan in the first week in February."

The last stage of the portage from Adamsfield to the river was accomplished by packing Hawkins' collapsible kayak into my fibreglass canoe, and sliding them both down the steep sides of the gorge. This was the easy way, but it didn't do much for my canoe. I had to put up with leaks from cracks in the fibreglass for the duration of the trip. Apart from that we were pleased with our lightweight craft. They were only about 3.4 metres long and made as light as possible, bearing in mind that, in view of Truchanas' experience, we expected to suffer the unenviable task of carrying these, and our gear, over the tops of the Splits, three narrow gorges created by breaks in a chain of hills. Truchanas had spent something like a fortnight accomplishing this task.

Hawkins' aluminium framed kayak was covered with heavy canvas. I used a fibreglass Canadian style canoe with four inflated car tubes, laid out lengthwise around the canoe and held in place by a canvas envelope attached to the gunwales. Before sealing both ends they were filled almost to capacity with foam plastic before being inserted into the envelope, the idea being to provide some buoyancy in the event of their being punctured. The modification worked well. The tubes made the canoe much more stable and, as a bonus, provided a cushion against rocks in the same manner as inflatable dinghies, or

Patterns in the water.

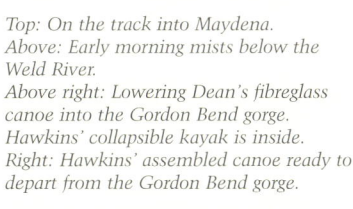

Top: On the track into Maydena.
Above: Early morning mists below the
Weld River.
Above right: Lowering Dean's fibreglass
canoe into the Gordon Bend gorge.
Hawkins' collapsible kayak is inside.
Right: Hawkins' assembled canoe ready to
depart from the Gordon Bend gorge.

'rubber duckies'. These have largely replaced canoes on the rougher rivers, because they are more forgiving of mistakes and are more versatile, particularly when portaging. This canoe is the only survivor from my trips. I lost three other craft.

A few days after setting off we encountered something which was quite unexpected. Paddling down a silent broadwater we became aware of raucous calls coming from somewhere downriver. As we drew closer the source of the noise became evident. A medium-sized Huon pine, leaning out over the water, began disgorging one cormorant after the other, and as they flew off their loud guttural calls of alarm filled the air. Closer still we could see that every suitable branch had a nest on it. This was a totally different habitat to the Franklin rookery at the beginning of Descension Gorge, where the nests were on cliff ledges. The one thing in common was that the hatchlings could drop straight down into the deep water. We climbed the tree to inspect them, and as we got close, some of the more advanced young panicked and jumped out of their nests into the river. They were a pathetic sight as they struggled and drowned, so we hurriedly climbed down and paddled away.

A smoke cloud in front of us, to the sought-west, was getting bigger.

Our next campsite was at the junction of the Wedge River, just above a rocky shoal. By now the sky was blotted out by a smoke haze, the sun appearing just above the horizon as a red ball reflected in the shallow water. I took a photo with the camp fire on rocks near the river in the foreground, not realising how useful this would be later.

Further downriver there were other surprises in store. The first occurred at the exit of the last Split. After lowering my canoe over a fall I happened to look back, and was amazed to see what looked like an eel leap up against the full force of water pouring upon it, and then cling to the vertical rockface. It progressed by propelling itself up a few inches at a time, hanging on, pausing, and then thrusting itself forward again. My base instinct said that this might be worth eating, so I pounced, and managed to hold it for a few seconds before it slipped out of my hands. That was long enough for me to see that it must have been a lamprey. Under its head was a large sucker. I have since learned that the lamprey is a parasite, and uses this to hang on while sharp teeth in its round mouth bite into its prey. The salivary glands produce a secretion which prevents coagulation of the victim's blood. Lampreys spend most of their lives at sea, and migrate up rivers to breed.

There was another time when I was more successful in catching something for the pot. We were eating breakfast close to the river when a small freshwater crayfish crawled up onto a rock ledge into the shallow water where we had thrown some scraps. It was quickly speared with a fork and dropped into an already boiling billy.

The upper Split. In this very dry spell, the water is still flowing beneath the boulders.

Finally, there was the mystery of the stinking eels. While paddling down a broadwater towards the end of the journey, we became aware of a strong fishy smell wafting upriver. We soon found the reason for it. Suspended on a dead branch of Huon pine, just above the water, were about a dozen eels in varying stages of decay. My first thought was that they must have been left stranded by a flood, but then I remembered the phrase 'as slippery as an eel', and came to the conclusion that no live eel would be caught up this way, so they must have been dead on arrival. But what killed them? Disease perhaps, or were they taken by cormorants in a time of plenty, and left for consumption in leaner times?

As was the case with the Franklin expedition, Hawkins carried a radio transceiver with which he could contact Hobart Radio. When it seemed that we no longer required a planned airdrop of food because we were ahead of schedule, this was cancelled. At the time this seemed a good idea. Then we were delayed by bad weather, and on the last day our food was down to two cups of rolled oats. It was a miserable day when we set off, and in spite of the rain the river was still low, so we had to ease our canoes over many shallows. Sometimes we would unexpectedly stumble into deep water up to our chests. Hawkins was getting ahead of me, with what seemed the greatest of ease, while I was struggling to keep up. Then, on looking back, I discovered the reason. I was dragging a tangled rope that had fallen off the stern of the canoe.

By this time I was cold, wet, hungry, exhausted and crabby and, deciding this was the last straw, called for a halt. We pulled up onto a low sandbank, and after several attempts, managed to get a fire burning. In order to save time, I didn't bother making a crane to hold the billy of water and just sat it on top of the sticks before adding the rolled oats. The porridge was coming along quite nicely when, without warning, the whole lot tipped over, spilling the contents over the sand! I could have cried! Without doubt this was the low point of an otherwise mostly enjoyable venture.

In one respect we were lucky on this trip. It was an exceptionally dry year, and we were able to go through the Gordon's three Splits rather than having to carry

A minor gorge.

everything over the top. Even so, there were treacherous portages, particularly in the first Split we encountered and the gorge above the Serpentine Junction where the river drops a few hundred metres in less than two kilometres. In places there was no water to be seen. You could only hear it gurgling under the huge boulders. Between gorges, long tranquil reaches, with minor rapids, offered respite from the strenuous portages, and once below the Serpentine junction, the only falls of any consequence were in the two other Splits. This was in contrast to the Franklin where, apart from the lower reaches, we were faced with one problem after another. Then again, if we had travelled lighter and been favoured with the fair weather we enjoyed most days on the Gordon, perhaps it would not have seemed so formidable. The Gordon was a river of extremes, but the good times outweighed the bad.

Some days after returning home I was visited by three detectives from Tasmania Police, who informed me that HEC employees who had been working in the middle Gordon area at about the same time that we passed through had reported that a fire raging there had spread from a campfire lit by us. I was able to produce the photo as evidence of fires already burning downstream from us, and point out that we had been careful about where we lit camp fires, always extinguishing them before departure. I thing they realised that the HEC were passing the buck. We heard nothing further about the matter.

Left: Sunset through smoke below the Wedge River.
Right: Travelling through the Gordon Bend gorge.

CHAPTER 9
PIEMAN RIVER—1964

Thrills
and spills

In the autumn of 1964 Olegas Truchanas, Peter
Dombrovskis, John Hawkins and I set out to canoe the
Pieman from the Murchison bridge at Tullah to Corinna,
twenty-two years before this enchanting river was to
disappear forever under the impoundment created by
the 122 metre high Reece Dam.

Above: Truchanas entering the rapids of the dolerite gorge.
Left: The Heemskirk Falls, now flooded by the Reece Dam. Dombrovskis in foreground.

On previous trips down the Pieman we did not have access to the river here as there was no road to Tullah, the only connection being by "Wee Georgie Wood" on its two foot gauge line.

Just above its junction with the Pieman there was a vertical drop of about eight feet (2.5 m) on the Murchison. We considered the possibility of shooting it but soon came to the conclusion that it was too risky. Then Olegas volunteered, "Do you want to get a good photo?" adding that if we did he would shoot it for us. At first I didn't take him seriously, but then it became obvious he was not bluffing. I should have tried to dissuade him against such a hazardous undertaking because I was not prepared to attempt it myself.

He paddled a short distance upstream, turned and pushed the canoe along as hard as he could to build up enough speed to carry him forward after plunging over the fall. But it was not enough. The canoe dived at a steep angle and the bow wedged itself on the bottom. It then rolled over, throwing him out. When he attempted to pull the canoe ashore his foot became jammed in a hole between rocks. While we watched helplessly from the other side of the river he struggled to free himself, and only finally succeeded by bending down underwater and twisting his foot free with his hands. Needless to say, none of us imitated his feat. Regretfully, the photos I took proved to be only record shots because he was too far away.

When we reached the dolerite gorge the river was in semi-flood, and before descending into the lower and fiercer of the rapids we were being swept along at great speed. You could easily be tipped out by the high waves, as indeed everyone was, except Dombrovskis, the novice of the trip. But you didn't have to worry too much about navigating over such a vast expanse of water and you could afford to take a look around.

I don't know who saw it first, but through a break in the rainforest someone caught a glimpse of falling water, back from the left bank. We hurriedly swung around, paddled back up to where a stream entered the river and landed to take a closer look. After rock-hopping for a short distance, we obtained an uninterrupted view of a magnificent spectacle: a huge waterfall about 20 metres high thundered down into a large pool at its base. These had to be the falls we had been warned about before setting off in 1951. Our anxiety

Top: Dombrovskis in his Truchanas-designed canoe.
Left: Truchanas.

would have been considerably lessened had we known beforehand that they were in fact not on the Pieman but a tributary, the Heemskirk River. This flows from Mt Heemskirk, the first landmark to be named by Tasman when he sighted Van Diemen's Land in 1642.

We couldn't resist the temptation to drag our canoes up the stream and photograph them in front of the Heemskirk Falls. Later, we could claim to have 'shot' this one!

RODE THE RAPIDS ON PIEMAN RIVER

The haunting beauty of the Pieman was too much to resist. In 1976 Stephanie and I and our son Geoff went back with Hawkins and his son Peter. This time it was a short journey from the Murchison bridge to Rosebery, which was probably just as well.

We noticed that Hawkins tired easily. One day he lowered his heavy canoe down the wrong branch of the river and then had to drag it back upstream. Looking tired and pale, he asked Stephanie, who was nearby, to give him a hand. That night he was keen to camp early. It should have been a warning but we tended to think he was just tired. As the only surgeon at the Alice Springs Hospital in the Northern Territory, his duties were demanding and the long hours of work were taking their toll.

Back in 1971, while standing on the beach at Lake Pedder admiring the indescribable beauty of the place, I discussed with Olegas Truchanas the possibility of saving the lake. He said, "We'll never save this lake, but we will save the Pieman."

That same year the Tasmanian Parliament approved the Pieman River Power Development and the conservation movement, still in its infancy, was unable to stop the destruction of either this magnificent river or Lake Pedder.

The next battle was to save the Franklin River.

Rubber duckies

Over thirty years after our first disastrous trip, I returned to the King River with my son Geoff. In contrast to last time we had a fun run through the gorge, mainly because we now used more suitable craft and travelled singly in two-man inflatable dinghies—the right size for one person and a pack.

Above: A new generation of adventurers and equipment: Geoff Dean rubber rafting in the King River gorge.
Opposite: Climbing heath (Prionotes cerinthoides) at the entrance to the gorge.

These 'rubber duckies' had been pioneered by Paul Smith and Bob Brown several years earlier on the Franklin. You could bungle through rapids sideways or backwards and still get away with it. Being inflatable, slamming into a rock was not necessarily a disaster—you usually bounced off without any serious damage to the raft or yourself. Portaging too was not the former hassle; they were easy to unload and carry upside down on your head and shoulders. However, we were still wary of logs for the reasons previously stated and, of course, any sharp snags.

This time we carried a detailed map and it indicated a waterfall emptying into the river near the end of the main gorge. This one was more secluded than the Heemskirk Falls just off the Pieman and we had to follow up a small stream flowing in from the right through a narrow chasm. We rounded a bend and there, suddenly before us, was an enchanting sight. The stream tumbled over the edge of a cliff into a crystal-clear, fern-edged pool some forty feet below. Unfortunately, when we stepped back far enough to include all the fall in a photograph our view was obstructed by a rock face.

Left: First campsite under Mt Owen.
Opposite: A young Huon pine grows at the water's edge.
Following pages: The middle of the King River gorge: what lies ahead?

Then followed an incident which I could well have done without. Late in the afternoon while being happily carried along by a swift current passing through a narrow gap between high rocks, I managed to foul both ends of the paddle against them. Before I had time to react the shaft of the paddle between my hands slammed back onto my face, knocking out a front tooth. To add insult to injury, Geoff chided me for being so clumsy!

Again this trip finished at the old Harris' Reward Track suspension bridge at the end of the gorge and from there we carried out the first load of gear, leaving this at Lynchford before proceeding to Queenstown, the first leg back to our vehicle parked with the caretaker at the King River picnic ground.

Still wearing our lifejackets because this was the easiest way to carry them we commenced to walk along the main street on the lookout for a lift back to our vehicle. It was a warm Saturday afternoon and the locals were imbibing on the footpath outside the pub. We immediately sensed hostility.

"It's not easy being a Greenie," they jeered. We didn't feel safe near them and walked down the middle of the road.

The campaign to save the Franklin had changed the mood in Queenstown.

The Franklin revisited

Nearly twenty years after the Franklin had been canoed for the first time, another generation of adventurers came of age.

Above: Portaging Newland Cascades in the rain.
Left: Rock Island Bend, lower Franklin.

My wife Stephanie and our children, Geoff, Malcolm and Annette, were eager to give it a go and find out if all I had told them about this fascinating, albeit demanding, river was true. John Gibb, the boys' art teacher at Kings Meadows High School in Launceston, agreed to come along too. This time we would avoid the troublesome upper Franklin and travel along a new access road from the Lyell Highway to the Hydro-Electric Commission's new Mt McCall camp at Propsting Gorge, the site of a second proposed Franklin River dam.

When Hawkins heard of our plans he couldn't wait to join us, and brought along his son Peter, who was a similar age to our two. Joe Scarlett, who had been with us on the disastrous 1951 attempt, joined us with his son Alan. The Scarlett family had been assisting Hawkins with his filming of the Franklin for some years. Both the Scarletts and Hawkins would use canoes. We had inflatable dinghies.

The HEC had recently built a haulageway down the sleep slope of Mt McCall into the gorge below, where they were carrying out investigations for a proposed dam. Hawkins came up with the idea of making use of this by sliding his heavy canoe down the five hundred metre drop, almost to the river. In order to control its descent down the steep railtrack Hawkins held it back with a nylon rope, one end of which was tied to the canoe, and the other end wrapped around a sleeper. All went well until friction between the rope and the sleeper produced enough heat for smoke to rise and the rope melted, allowing the canoe to have a mind of its own. It hurtled off down the haulageway, and it seemed that its headlong flight would only cease when it finished up in small pieces at the bottom. Fortunately it veered off to one side and crashed into bushes, which brought it to a gradual stop with little damage. After this near disaster, we thought it wise to carry our inflatable rafts down the slippery track rather than try something similar.

That night we camped on a sand bank a few miles downstream. We set off before the Hawkins and the Scarletts, expecting them to follow soon afterwards.

Towards the end of the day, with the river rising from constant rain, we were all drenched, from above and below. Wetsuits were unheard of, and the best we could do was wear wool jumpers, parkas and shorts, and even if we started off dry, seated on an inflated lilo on the floor of our dinghy, it wasn't long before we were sitting in a pool of water.

A high wave hit Gibbie's raft and he was thrown out, together with his pack. The rope tying this to the dinghy wound itself around his ankle, pulling him down and preventing him from climbing back into his craft. Not realising his predicament, I was yelling at him to get back in because there was a rough stretch coming up, but he didn't seem to be hearing above the noise of the water. The fact that he was partially deaf did not help. But he extricated himself successfully.

We came to a sizeable fall, which normally we would have checked before shooting. Since we couldn't get any wetter, I decided to take a chance and plunged over, and the other four followed. Now thoroughly saturated, I thought it worth continuing on to a cavern I remembered seeing just before the Gaylard Rapids in 1959, which might provide some shelter. As it turned out, we were not only out of the weather but were able to thaw out around a roaring fire, fed by dry driftwood that had been washed into the wide mouth of the cavern. After getting into dry clothes and gorging ourselves on hot food we were new people. We cleared away the small rocks lying on top of the sand to make a platform to lie on. Stephanie and I even had our own apartment next door, a cave just big enough for two. All in all, it was a home away from home!

What had happened to the others? Gibbie and I set off to find out. We had walked less than a kilometre upstream when we were confronted with an overhanging cliff face. To get over this we had to bash through thick wet scrub. When we reached the top we hollered out with all our might. There was no answer. They must have been further upriver than we imagined. We retreated to our shelter, hoping they would turn up, but they didn't. Apparently Hawkins and Scarlett had decided to call it a day and had chosen to camp under an overhanging rockface. Nevertheless it was not a dry campsite like ours, and in fact they had a miserable time. We delayed our departure for a day waiting for them to join us. When they didn't we were not

Gibb's goof after hitting high wave!

unduly concerned as Hawkins had indicated that they would not be hurrying because he needed good weather to do some filming. This was my busy time of the year and I had to get back to my job as an irrigation specialist, even though under the circumstances it was hard to imagine anywhere that would need water!

The weather had scarcely improved as we headed off next morning, lining the first part of the Gaylard Rapids and portaging around the 'widowmaker' at the Pig Trough. Drifting past Rock Island, a long-tailed water-rat scurried up the almost vertical rockface. We portaged the Newland Cascades in misty rain, and pushed on to the Jane River Hut for the night.

It was wet and freezing cold by the time we reached Double Fall the following day. Further downriver a pair of sea eagles soared majestically overhead. We passed the impressive Galleon Bluff, which resembles several Spanish ships in dock, their sterns jutting out into the placid dark water. Approaching the overhanging Verandah Cliffs the children started shouting, and their calls echoed far upstream; they considered The Sound Shell would have been a better name. In these lower reaches the river was now much wider and slower.

After several days of natural sounds the peace was suddenly shattered by the noise of a helicopter which landed a working party on a rocky shoal near us, and then barely cleared our heads as it took off. Later, a pile driver with its constant thuds echoed across the water, and an HEC camp was visible in the bush; preliminary tests for dam building had commenced.

It was still raining as we crossed Macquarie Harbour in the tourist launch. Only when the vessel arrived at Strahan did we see the sun. Looking inland, we could see that menacing dark clouds still hung over the Franklin River area.

Shortly after his trip was over Scarlett left for a tour of New Zealand with his wife Kath. He felt unwell, and was only able to keep going by visiting doctors and chemist shops along the way. Back in Melbourne his son John, now a doctor, ordered him into hospital, where he was diagnosed as having a blood disorder.

When he reached Launceston Hawkins was bedridden with rheumatic fever, and spent several days recovering. In early September 1979 he took a short time off from his heavy workload at the Alice Springs Hospital to do some filming in Katherine Gorge with the idea of adding this to the Franklin River film by way of comparison. With his wife he climbed up to the lookout. On returning he collapsed and died from a sudden heart attack.

Once on the Franklin he had remarked, "This river could claim one of us before we finish!"

In a way, the river claimed him.

Opposite: Malcolm, John and Annette Dean at the Verandah Cliffs.

POSTSCRIPT

I didn't realise it at the time but Hawkins must have been just as moved by the magnificent scenery at Transcendence Reach as I was. In later years he mentioned to his wife that, if possible, his ashes be scattered on top of the hill at the junction of the Livingston and Franklin rivers.

On a clear, frosty September morning in 1979, twenty years after the first descent of the Franklin, John Hawkins' wife Kay and I boarded a light aircraft at Western Junction and set off to fulfil John's wish.

Leaving the patchwork of agricultural land behind we climbed over the snow covered peaks of the Western Tiers and headed southwest. Below lay the vast expanse of Great Lake, then to our right innumerable small lakes and tarns appeared in endless succession amidst the snow. Next, Lake St Clair, surrounded by rugged peaks and then on to towering Frenchmans Cap. From there we turned south and followed the Livingston River to our destination.

After the pilot had selected the best approach through the hills, we dropped John's ashes above the white quartz landmark which we now call Hawkins Blaze.

His name is further perpetuated in the Northern Territory where a street in Alice Springs and the new operating theatre at the hospital are named after him, as well as a Royal Flying Doctor Service aircraft.

He was made a Fellow of the Royal Australasian College of Surgeons in 1973 and later awarded an M.B.E. for services to the community.

Above: Hawkins and Dean. Right: Hawkins Blaze.

This was the end of an era. The following years would see a battle between forces intent on destroying this wild river and conservationists who were determined that it should be saved for future generations to enjoy.

The Franklin River was eventually saved, but the Pieman, King and upper Gordon were lost to posterity.

When we set forth to 'conquer' the Franklin, it was evident that the HEC was very interested in damming it and, I have to confess, my feeling at the time was that once the all-powerful HEC decided to go ahead there was little I could do to stop it. Then after it had more than once nearly claimed my life I was less inclined to be concerned about its future. My thinking was that it was a dangerous river and others should not be exposed to the same risks.

Then gradually my attitude changed as it became more obvious that our own foolishness was more often than not the cause of misadventure.

It took imaginative adventurers like Dr Bob Brown and Paul Smith to demonstrate that the outcome could be quite different with the right approach and proper planning. They showed that, rather than being a formidable challenge, the experience could be made both enjoyable and exhilarating. They even found time to name the outstanding features.

Rubber duckies (inflatable rafts) proved much more suitable for the conditions. Where we were often in serious trouble with canoes, duckies were much more forgiving of mistakes and, if we decided to bypass a hazardous rapid, they were far easier to portage than had been our heavy kayaks. Diehard canoeists turned to using lightweight fibreglass kayaks with great success.

The King, the Pieman, the Franklin, the Gordon. Of these four great rivers in Tasmania's western wilderness only one, the Franklin, still runs undammed to the sea.

Looking back, despite all the hardships for me and my companions, I was most fortunate to live at a time when it was still possible to canoe these wild and remote rivers, now lost to adventurers forever.

Opposite: Franklin River names and distances compiled by Dr Bob Brown.
Many of these features were named by Brown and Smith.

REFERENCES

1   Garry Kerr & Harry McDermott, *The Huon Pine Story*, Portland, Vic. 1999. p72

2   Geoffrey Blainey, *The Peaks of Lyell*, Melbourne, Vic. 1967. p10

3   Charles Whitham, *Western Tasmania*, Hobart, Tas. 1923. p16

4   C.J. Binks, *Explorers of Western Tasmania*. Launceston,Tas. 1980. p28

5   ibid p253

6   Richard Flanagan, *A Terrible Beauty*, Richmond, Vic. 1985 Foreword by Bob Brown, p v

7   Marcus Clark, *For the Term of His Natural Life*, Springvale, Vic. 2000. p97

8   C.J. Binks, *Explorers of Western Tasmania*, Launceston 1980. p153

9   Garry Kerr & Harry McDermott, op. cit. p78

10 Dr John Hawkins as told to Harry Frauca, "Canoe Saga", *Australian Outdoors*, Aug. 1959.

11 C.J. Binks, op. cit. p153

12 Peter Griffiths & Bruce Walker, *The Ever Varying Flood: a guide to the Franklin River*, Richmond, Vic. 1997. p4

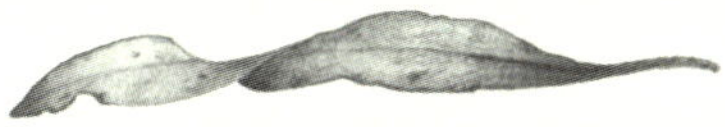

FRANKLIN RIVER: 121 Km in length.

COLLINGWOOD BRIDGE TO

COLLINGWOOD - FRANKLIN JUNCTION	5·0 Km
LODDON JUNCTION	9·0 km
IRENABYSS	16·5 km
FINCHAM CROSSING	24·0 Km
TOP OF (INCEPTION REACH) GREAT RAVINE	49·0
ANDREW RIVER	56·5
ROCK ISLAND BEND	64·0
JANE RIVER	71·0
DOUBLE FALL.	85.0
BIG FALL.	89·5
GORDON RIVER (PYRAMID ISL)	96·0
BUTLER ISLAND	104·0
MARBLE CLIFFS.	107·0 Km.

INDEX